"Hicks remembers it all with immense charm, wit, and brio, capturing a bygone world of country estates, glass cigarette holders kept in a petticoat pocket, sapphire-studded powder compacts, dials on bedroom doors turned to indicate when you'd like to be woken with tea and biscuits, and enough pets to populate an exotic zoo."

—*The Daily Beast*

## Praise for *Daughter of Empire*

"Lady Pamela presents an honest yet blithe portrayal of her famous, eccentric family and offers a glimpse into the inner circle of Britain's royalty."

—*The Washington Post*

"For its historical sweep and its uniquely vantaged window onto many important moments of the middle of the last century, *Daughter of Empire* is something for *Downton* fans—and even others interested in England, class, and monarchy—to look out for."

—*The Buffalo News*

"The story of Lady Hicks, who lived the kind of life we think of as only existing in books and movies, with nannies, governesses, and all the trappings of the English elite. . . . Many fans of *Downton Abbey* will certainly enjoy it."

—*Kirkus Reviews*

"Pamela Mountbatten has had a front-row seat at many extraordinary historical events and, as this wonderfully entertaining memoir shows, the privilege has not been wasted on her. Her wry, intimate portraits of royals, politicians, and Hollywood stars are a joy to read."

—*Zoë Heller*

"Lady Pamela's memoir will appeal to those who like to take a peek into the lifestyles of the royal and famous. Underneath the glamour and glitz, this brief autobiography has a bit more substance, since Hicks was . . . an eyewitness to and a participant in some of the most momentous events of the twentieth century."

—*Booklist*

"A life filled with celebrity-like happenings delivered with impeccable taste. Revealing, yet properly reserved."

—*Historical Novels Review*

"This is a book which will give pleasure to everyone who reads it."

—Lady Antonia Fraser

"Imagine *Downton Abbey* meets Oscar Wilde. Now read *Daughter of Empire: My Life as a Mountbatten* by Pamela Hicks, one of the most intimate accounts of turbulent domestic life in the shadow of world-altering events. . . . Two beautiful people, many continents, World War II, lots of distractions, and even more namedropping. . . . What's not to love?"

—*India Today*

"A glance at court life from the Mountbatten perspective. . . . Lady Pamela's portrait of her upbringing by two remarkable parents is affectionate and spirited."

—*The Daily Telegraph*

"A jolly romp."

—*Tatler*

"A uniquely intimate glimpse of the queen few really know. In this captivating memoir, her cousin reveals a playful and surprisingly emotional woman."

—*Daily Mail*

"She writes . . . with charm, geniality, and a sense of humor."

—*The Spectator*

ALSO BY LADY PAMELA HICKS

*India Remembered* (as Pamela Mountbatten)

# Daughter
## *of* Empire

## My Life as a Mountbatten

## LADY PAMELA HICKS

SIMON & SCHUSTER PAPERBACKS

NEW YORK   LONDON   TORONTO   SYDNEY   NEW DELHI

Simon & Schuster Paperbacks
A Division of Simon & Schuster, Inc.
1230 Avenue of the Americas
New York, NY 10020

First Simon & Schuster trade paperback edition September 2014
Originally published in Great Britain in 2012 by Weidenfeld & Nicolson

SIMON & SCHUSTER PAPERBACKS and colophon are registered trademarks
of Simon & Schuster, Inc.

For information about special discounts for bulk purchases, please contact Simon &
Schuster Special Sales at 1-866-506-1949 or business@simonandschuster.com.

The Simon & Schuster Speakers Bureau can bring authors to your live event. For
more information or to book an event contact the Simon & Schuster Speakers
Bureau at 1-866-248-3049 or visit our website at www.simonspeakers.com.

*Designed by Akasha Archer*

Manufactured in the United States of America

10 9 8 7 6 5 4 3 2 1

The Library of Congress has cataloged the hardcover edition as follows:
Hicks, Pamela, 1929–
    Daughter of empire : my life as a Mountbatten / Lady Pamela Hicks.—First
Simon & Schuster edition.
        pages cm
    "Originally published in Great Britain in 2012 by Weidenfeld & Nicolson"—T.p.
verso.
    Includes bibliographical references and index.
    1. Hicks, Pamela, 1929–  2. Upper class women—Great Britain—Biography.
    3. Upper class—Great Britain—Biography.  4. Ladies-in-waiting—Great Britain—
Biography.  I. Title.
    DA591.H47A3 2013
    941.082092—dc23
    [B]

                                                                2013008889

ISBN 978-1-4767-3381-4
ISBN 978-1-4767-3382-1 (pbk)
ISBN 978-1-4767-3383-8 (ebook)

*For Edwina and Ashley and India,*
*with my love*

# Daughter
## *of* Empire

# I

My father could trace his roots back to the ninth century. Through forty-one generations, he was able to recount the lives of our ancestors—royalists, rebels, and saints. He never tired of telling me that it was extremely rare for a family to be able to cite two canonized antecedents. "The first," he would say proudly, "goes way back to the thirteenth century. St. Elisabeth of Hungary was a gracious princess who secretly gave alms to the poor. Her husband didn't approve of this and, one morning, ordered her to remove the cover of her basket. And"—I loved the ending of this story—"her forbidden bread had miraculously turned into roses.

"The other was your great-aunt Ella, Grand Duchess Serge of Russia, who, following her husband's assassination, became a nun and worked tirelessly among the poor and sick of Moscow. In 1918, when she, the chief nun, three young princes, a grand duke, and a lady-in-waiting were thrown down a mine shaft by the Bolsheviks—along with a few hand grenades for good measure—witnesses heard her clear sweet voice singing 'Hail Gentle Light' and other hymns of fortitude to her fellow victims. Before she died, she tore up her nun's veil to provide bandages for the princes' wounds."

Now known as St. Elisabeth of Romanova, my great-aunt

is one of twelve modern saints preserved in sculpture above the West Door of Westminster Abbey. It was hard to keep track of my father's long line of relatives, but as he loved lists and charts and stories, he was always ready to bring them to life. For many generations his ancestors had been rulers of the Grand Duchy of Hesse in Germany, a landlocked territory far from the coast. It was his father, Prince Louis Alexander of Battenberg, who changed all that and altered the course of the family's path. In 1868, at the tender age of fourteen, beset by dreams of a seafaring life, he surprised everyone by announcing that he was leaving home to set sail. In fact he was so determined to become part of the "greatest navy in the world" that he took British citizenship, eventually rising to the top job of First Sea Lord and Admiral of the Fleet. He didn't cut off his ties with Europe completely, though, falling in love with his cousin Princess Victoria of Hesse, a sparky, independent-minded granddaughter of Queen Victoria, who was related to most of the royal courts in Europe. In those days it wasn't always an advantage to have family members scattered across Europe, and during the First World War his mother found herself on opposite sides to her brother and sister. Luckily, my father always said, while patriotism was intense, it never undermined strong family affections.

My grandparents married in 1884 and lived variously in England, Germany, and Malta. My father, also Prince Louis of Battenberg but known as "Dickie," was born in 1900, the youngest of four children. The aging Queen Victoria held him at his christening and he wriggled so much that he got her full square in the face with a fist and a foot, knocking off her spectacles. He always told me that at only a few weeks old, he couldn't possibly have known he was to be "seen and not heard" while in the queen's arms.

My father was blessed with enlightened parents. His mother in particular thought that children should not only be seen and very much heard but that they should also be exposed to new ideas and the classics. She kept meticulous records of the books she read and was always keen to try new experiences. Passionate about cartography, she worked for many years on a detailed geological map of Malta, participated in archaeological digs, and rather daringly, scooping up my father to provide the required extra weight, flew in a zeppelin airship and a very early model of a biplane, even though, as she said, "it was not made to carry passengers and we perched securely on a little stool holding on to the flier's back." Coming from a line of progressive thinkers, she taught my father herself until he was ten years old, gifting him an education that was thorough and polymathic. She taught him to be open-minded, methodical, and thorough, and above all encouraged him to enjoy learning, to inquire. Later, when I got to know my grandmother, I could see how entirely free of prejudice she was, how *interested* she was in all that was around her, and just how much of an influence she had had on my father's refreshing way of viewing the world. She was to be an inspiring force in my life.

A month before his tenth birthday my father was sent to Lockers Park prep school in Hertfordshire, and two years later he entered the Royal Naval College at Osborne. As war became inevitable, at the beginning of 1914, his German-born father was forced to retire from the Admiralty as first sea lord because of the anti-German hysteria at large in the country, scurrilous newspaper headlines whipping people up into a frenzy of hatred. My grandfather resigned, even though the navy was solidly behind him, and this episode had a profound effect on my father, who vowed to succeed to the position of his wronged father. Then, during the war, when King George V decreed that the royal family should anglicize their name, choosing Windsor, my grandfather changed his from Battenberg to Mountbatten. The king created him the Marquess of Milford Haven, having offered him the title of duke, but, practical to the last and looking around him at the grandeur of the English nobility, he calculated that as his savings had been decimated in the German economic downturn, he simply didn't have the wealth that would be expected of him with that rank: an English duke had to maintain a grand style of life. My father also ceased to be the younger Prince Louis of Battenberg and received the courtesy title of Lord Louis Mountbatten.

During the First World War, my father joined Lord Beatty's flagship HMS *Lion* as a midshipman, and later he was appointed first lieutenant of a small ship, HMS *P31,* and for a time, aged only eighteen, he found himself in command of a crew of sixty. Through Princess Mary my father contrived that King George V should come on board during the Peace Pageant on the Thames. He saluted smartly as the monarch came aboard. "Hello, Dickie," said the king jovially, "how's Chicken Bella?" The fact that his sovereign remembered the stupid doll he had had as a two-year-old mortified the nineteen-year-old second in command and exposed him to remorseless teasing.

The Admiralty now sent the "war babies" who had been unable to complete their education to Cambridge University, and my father went with both Prince Albert and Prince Henry. They all led a wildly social life, falling in and out of love between studying. Tall, with the good looks of a Hollywood film star, my father was very much in demand. He was also in demand from the royal household, accompanying the Prince of Wales—the future King Edward VIII—as his personal aide-de-camp, on tours including Australia and, later, India and Japan.

Grace Kelly once confided that she had always kept a photograph of my father before she met Prince Rainier. Mrs. Cornelius Vanderbilt, a fiercely rich American society hostess, nicknamed "the Kingfisher" for her relentless cultivation of European royalty, singled my father out as the perfect suitor for her only daughter. When she invited him to a tea party on her yacht off Cowes, my father was immediately smitten, falling helplessly in love at first sight. Only it wasn't quite as Mrs. Vanderbilt had intended, for on board that afternoon was a gathering of young ladies, including Edwina Ashley, an effortlessly glamorous heiress, who had recently learned to stand with her hips pushed slightly forward, the very image of beau monde chic. With one hand on her slender hip, the charms of her gold bracelet glinting off the other in the sun, my father was at once dazzled and delighted. Although they had met a couple of times previously, they began to court in earnest, and when my father went to India with the prince, Edwina followed him, staying at the Viceregal Lodge. It became obvious to all that they were very much in love, so much so that the Prince of Wales lent them his sitting room so that my father could propose.

On 18 July 1922, they were married in St. Margaret's, Westminster, tucked in the shadow of Westminster Abbey on Parliament Square. It was the most talked-about society wedding of the year, and when my mother walked out on the arm of her dashing husband, beneath a naval arch of swords, they were congratulated by a host of royals, including King George V, Queen Mary, and the Queen Mother, Alexandra. At the sumptuous reception, the Prince of Wales gave the best man's speech, following which my parents enjoyed a rather protracted honeymoon, traveling to France, Spain, Germany, and the States, where they stayed with Hollywood's royalty, the king and queen of silent movies, Mary Pickford and Douglas Fairbanks. They even made a short silent home movie with Charlie Chaplin entitled *Nice and Easy*, in which Charlie played a rogue trying to steal the pearls of the heroine (my mother), who is rescued by her lover (my father). My mother's performance showed suitable girlish alarm, my father's acting was dreadful, and of course Charlie stole the show. Happily exhausted, they returned to Manhattan for the last days of their adventure, where they stayed as guests of the very game Mrs. Cornelius Vanderbilt, who bore no grudges.

Marriage, my father's love, and a sense of her own destiny—this is just what my mother needed. Since her "coming out" she had been living with her grandfather, Sir Ernest Cassell, in his London home, Brook House, stoically hosting his large parties of elderly grandees and financiers, but his death in the year before her marriage had left my mother feeling empty, memories of her lonely childhood flooding back to her. Raised by a series of nannies and housekeepers in Broadlands, a large Palladian mansion near Romsey in Hampshire, Edwina and her younger sister, Mary, were mostly kept apart from their parents. Her mother, Maudie, suffered from consumption and, as her condition deteriorated, she spent more and more time away, particularly in Egypt. Their father, Wilfred, a Conservative MP, was rarely at home either, busy attending to his political duties. My mother's early letters show how anxious she was to see her "darling mother" again. Having been misled by a well-intentioned suggestion from their governess, my mother believed that the reason for their separation was that she was going to be a sister again, and she wrote to her mother at least twice expressing her and Mary's desire to have a little brother. After a while the penny dropped and she tried to keep the desperation out of her letters, going out of her way to keep her tone upbeat. When Maudie finally returned to Broadlands, it was thought too upsetting for the children to witness their mother's failing health, so they were sent away to a cousin. And even though my mother wrote several times with growing urgency and despair, pleading to see her mother again, she was never allowed to, and Maudie died in February 1911. My mother and Mary did not attend the funeral.

My mother was brave, hiding her emotions well, containing her sister, who became very difficult, throwing tantrums and creating scenes. It seemed that she was the only one who could calm Mary down, and forever after, she felt responsible for her younger sister's safety and well-being. A subdued period of existence followed, during which time the girls learned to pour their bruised feelings into caring for a menagerie of domestic pets—puppies, ponies, rabbits, kittens, and a goat. For a brief while, their lives were cheered and enriched by the arrival of Laura Deveira, a loving young governess to whom the sisters became deeply attached, but just as they began to settle down and come out of their protective shells, their father presented them with a new stepmother and the world came crashing down again.

Molly Forbes-Sempill replaced their beloved Miss Deveira with a governess of her choice and sent the girls to bed every evening by half past six so they were "out of the way," a phrase that deeply upset my mother. My mother and aunt were forbidden to pick a single flower from the garden from the moment she moved in, and Broadlands became a sterile and difficult place in which to live. Eventually my mother went to school near Eastbourne—another lonely place for her—where the pupils took it in turns "hooking up Miss Potts," a humiliating task involving wrestling with endless hooks and buttons in order to help the headmistress secure her dress each morning. Things improved little more when, aged eighteen, my mother was sent to a domestic science training college. It was while here that she vowed never to go back and live at Broadlands while her stepmother was alive. On leaving she went to live in London with her grandfather, Sir Ernest.

Life changed for the better when she met my father. They had both been recently touched by death—my father distraught at the loss of his father, my mother by the unexpected death of her grandfather—and initially they sought solace in each other. As time passed, however, and finally freed from her past, rich from her inheritance (which included Brook House), and happily in love, my mother found life opening up for her. This was the beginning of the "roaring twenties," a time of exuberance and great optimism: jazz, dance, and liberating new styles. My mother was fashionably slender— she referred to herself as a "straight actress" with vital statistics of twenty-six all the way down—and she took full advantage of the freedom afforded to women now that bustles and corsets were obstructions of the past. She soon cut her hair short à la mode and kept it immaculately coiffed. As hemlines rose and shoes became more prominent, my mother had hers handmade in Paris, a pair in every color. This was the extravagant time in my parents' lives—they had a cinema screen installed in Brook House and hosted regular parties at which princes, even kings and queens, could rub shoulders with the likes of Noël Coward, Cole Porter, and George

Gershwin. By playing it at her parties, my mother made "The Man I Love" an overnight hit in England after Gershwin told her how upset he was that it had flopped in the United States. She danced the Charleston with Fred Astaire, and the rumors that Queen Mary didn't approve of this kind of behavior made the dancing all the more delicious.

If they weren't entertaining at home, my parents went out to clubs, and it was only when they arrived that the party really got started. Once they had danced into the early hours, they would return to Brook House, music ringing in their ears, and collapse into bed. As was the fashion in those days, they kept separate bedrooms—my father's decorated to look like a ship's cabin, a porthole in the wall with an ingenious "view" of Malta built behind. He had designed the light switch himself so that when turned down it emitted a low hum, like that of a ship's engine, and this helped him get to sleep. The walls were pale green and the carpet black, the bed was covered in a thick orange cotton quilt handwoven in Malta—this much I know because it would be the same wherever we lived thereafter. My mother slept next door between pink satin sheets with a swan's-down quilt covered in pink ostrich feathers so that it appeared to float.

During the first months of their marriage, while my father was waiting for the completion of the ship to which he had been assigned, he and my mother continued to enjoy a busy social life, playing golf, lunching with friends, partying in the evenings. On the weekends, they would escape to Adsdean, a rented house, not far from Portsmouth, where they would entertain friends, take walks in the country, and show off their rather exotic collection of animals, which over time came to include a lion cub, two wallabies, a bush baby, and a coatimundi, a kind of anteater named Shnozzle. Being rich and lavish in their hospitality in both town and country meant that they depended on a large body of staff, the majority of whom traveled up and down between London and Sussex in the staff bus.

They were certainly kept busy, seeing to the needs of the various guests, some of whom visited as often as my parents. Peter Murphy was a particular favorite, bringing laughter and fun into any room he entered. Peter ran a left-wing bookshop and once gave my mother a book on raising children that she never picked up but which my father devoured and tried to follow to the best of his abilities. Peter's jacket and trouser pockets were always stuffed with newspaper and periodical cuttings that he would dish out to relevant recipients as if they were sweets. He was a brilliant thinker, engaging my parents and their various guests in pithy debates; he spoke several languages fluently, was famed for his hilarious mimicry, and could play any tune on the piano by ear.

Another regular visitor was Paula Long. She was a great beauty, painted by Augustus John and much photographed by Cecil Beaton. In the 1920s she wore white face powder and any "deb's delight" worth his salt wanted to be seen to have white powder on his jacket shoulder, a sign that he had danced with her. Her married life was turbulent and she had an assortment of husbands: the Marquis de Casa Maury, a racing driver and founder of the Curzon Cinema, with whom she led a very social life; Bill Allen, a keen backpacker with whom she trekked across Europe; and Boy Long, a tea planter in Kenya, where she lived in the world of the "Happy Valley" set. Later, when my mother became serious and put these days behind her, Paula was the only friend she kept from this wild period of her life.

As time went on, my father's naval duties often took him

away from my mother. She was bored alone—her childhood demons coming to haunt her—and so became increasingly reliant on her loyal "ginks" or admirers for entertainment. She began to collect young men in a way that raised many eyebrows. Now that she had control over her life, this kind of chase became exciting. Of course, the ramifications were messy and complex—when my father first heard that my mother had taken a lover, he was devastated, but eventually, using their reserves of deep mutual affection, my parents managed to negotiate a way through this crisis and found a modus vivendi. On a lighter note, my mother's social life presented the staff with its own problems. Brook House was large, but even it could not provide enough rooms to ensure that no young man was aware of the others. When my mother returned from shopping one day she was met with "Mr. Larry Gray is in the drawing room, Mr. Sandford is in the library, Mr. Ted Philips is in the boudoir, Señor Portago in the anteroom, and I don't know what to do with Mr. Molyneux." It was my father's complete lack of jealousy and total desire for my mother's happiness that made their marriage work.

My mother longed to see the world. From an early age, possibly symptomatic of a repressed desire to flee her childhood, she had slept with a pocket atlas by her bed. So when my father's job afforded her the opportunity to travel, she caught the bug. From then on, she was often away for long periods and for a while was not in England for more than a few weeks at a time. Even in 1924, when my sister, Patricia, was born, she partied in the South of France, leaving her baby daughter at home at just a month old. It seemed that she couldn't stop herself indulging in this hedonistic way of life, the endless adventure and travel that so thrilled her.

Fortunately my father was devoted to his new baby daughter from the moment she was born, a bond that was to last his lifetime and one that would extend to include me.

My birth caused a good deal of trouble. When my father's tour of naval duty in Malta came to an end, my parents and two naval friends set off for five days in Morocco. My mother, normally so sprightly, was pregnant with me, although it hardly showed. When my father had asked his C in C for some time off he had been told, "Pull the other one, Dickie! Don't try that old sailor's excuse with me; I only danced with your wife last night!"

From Morocco, they crossed to Gibraltar so my father could return to his ship, HMS *Revenge*, for combined maneuvers of the Mediterranean and Atlantic fleets. Never one to miss out, my mother had made plans for the time he was away: the chauffeur had driven her beloved Hispano-Suiza H6 from England and, roaring out of town, in the front seat, in neat cloche hat, dark glasses, flawlessly rouged lips, and bright red nails, she felt on top of the world. As they climbed the mountains towards Málaga, however, the twists and turns left my mother feeling sick and exhausted, as did the train journeys onward through to Madrid and Barcelona. Finally making her weary way to the polo club to meet up with my father, who had come to join her and play in a tournament, she was all but finished off. After the match my parents went straight to their suite at the Ritz. In the early hours of Friday, 19 April 1929, my mother awoke with severe contractions. I was on my way.

Despite my father's best efforts, the hotel could only find an ear, nose, and throat specialist to help them. In desperation my father telephoned his cousin Queen Ena, in Madrid. She was away, but King Alfonso answered. "We're having a baby," exclaimed my father. The king, a great womanizer, got the wrong end of the stick and replied, "Oh, my dear Dickie, I won't tell anyone." "Tell everyone!" implored my father. "It's my *wife*. Edwina's having the baby." "Leave everything to me," said the king, and rang off. Within half an hour the Royal Guard had the hotel surrounded. In the meantime a doctor had been found and dispatched to the local hospital to secure the necessary equipment and an English nurse, who appeared "like an angel" and administered chloroform to deaden the pain my mother was experiencing. Downstairs, the doctor had returned from the hospital with an ominously large bag, but he rushed with such steely determination towards the entrance of the hotel that he was promptly arrested by the Royal Guards.

My mother was by now hemorrhaging, so was unaware of the events that began to unfold beyond the hotel walls with the slapstick absurdity of one of my father's favorite Buster Keaton movies. As the commotion in and around the hotel reached fever pitch, in Nice my parents' great friend Peter Murphy had been roused at dawn by my father's anguished phone call. He grabbed his driver and set off immediately. They drove nonstop for twenty-four hours, Peter telling endless stories to keep his driver awake, something that eventually began to tax even his brilliant skills as a raconteur, not to mention his driver's ability to remain attentive for so long.

In the early hours of the morning Peter and his driver finally entered Barcelona at such speed that they crashed, yards from the hotel, into a tram. Panting and bleeding, Peter hotfooted it up the stairs of the Ritz and burst into the room, shaken but triumphant. As heads turned away from my mother, someone shouted at him to "get off the carpet."

Then all eyes turned back to me. I had arrived safely and

was wrapped in a beautifully embroidered layette that had been brought in by some local nuns. I lay in a crib made from a little dog basket: a solitary, happy presence, blissfully unaware of the noise and tumult of the family life into which I had just been delivered.

## 2

It unsettles me how I can remember some elements of my early childhood with astonishing clarity while other, more important memories remain blurred, hazy images in my mind. For example, I can remember the long woolen gaiters I was made to wear as a child and my nanny's crooked front tooth, but I cannot remember my mother ever spending any length of time with me in Adsdean, our old, rambling house near the Sussex Downs.

As a young child I rarely saw my mother. During the day Nanny Vera looked after me in the first-floor tower room nursery. She was the center of my world and occupied me for hours: playing with me, taking me for walks, knitting clothes for my dolls, and generally being my champion. I was kept away from my sister, Patricia, for most of the day so that she could concentrate on her lessons in the schoolroom with her governess, Miss Vick—Vicky. At least, that was one reason. The other reason was that Nanny and Vicky did not get on at all, were constantly at war about this or that, and therefore it was only at teatime that my sister and I were allowed to play together downstairs. We were always pleased to see each other and had a number of imaginative games on the go, a rich make-believe world of our own.

The highlight of my day was getting ready for bed. As I went through each stage—having a bath, getting into my nightdress, brushing my teeth—I would start to buzz with excitement at the thought that one of my parents would come and visit me before I went off to sleep. My father loved to read or tell me stories, his voice mellifluous and comforting, and I would lie in a state of bliss as I drifted off to the sound of his words. And if my mother were in the country she would come in and say good night before she went out. I would listen out for the tinkling of the charms on her bracelet and after she had leant down and kissed me, I would lie awake and savor her scent for as long as it lingered in my bedroom.

Sadly, my mother and my nanny got in the way of my father's bedtime stories, for when I was about five he started to read *Prenez Garde à la Peinture*, in French. Nanny, who always wanted me to herself, had complained that it was making me upset as I didn't understand what he was saying, and that gave Mummy the ammunition she needed. She was unhappy that Patricia fiercely adored my father and she didn't like it that he and I had this special ritual. Suddenly he stopped reading to me at bedtime. I knew he was very busy with his work, but for a time I was bereft, marooned and uncomprehending.

For all this, though, Patricia and I never felt unloved. We were caught up in our everyday life at Adsdean—our dogs and our ponies and the marvelous outdoors. I loved Nanny fiercely and we both adored our housekeeper, Mrs. Lankaster, known as Hanky, who gave us engulfing, warm hugs. We were also favorites of the housemaids, Jessie and Dorothy. When Patricia was about eight, the height of her ambition was to be like Jessie. She commandeered a feather duster and followed her from room to room, intent on learning, taking in every detail of how and what to dust. She watched longingly as Jessie made up the fires, frustrated that she could not help. I harbored no such ambition and was more fascinated by an ivory-colored dial on the door of the bedrooms which guests could alter to indicate what time they would like to be woken with tea and biscuits and have their curtains pulled back. I studied the dials intently and longed for the day when I would be tall enough to turn them myself.

All this is not to say that we didn't have a family life. We did—when my parents were at home—and on these special days we would all spend a great deal of time together outdoors, having lunch or playing with the Sealyhams. Patricia and I would take our parents by the hand and lead them to our own little garden, where we had planted seeds and labeled them. We would hold our breath, hoping that something might have grown or flowered so that we could impress our parents. Patricia was allowed to go riding with my father—that is, until she fell off Fairy and broke her arm—and we all enjoyed going for long walks with the dogs.

There was, of course, a constant stream of guests and visitors, which made our house buzz with life. In spite of, or perhaps because of, his best efforts at my birth, King Alfonso of Spain had become my godfather. Back then godparents were not expected to take much, if any, interest after the christening of their charge, and many didn't. Carmen, Duchess of Peñaranda, for instance (after whom I acquired my middle name), had been a good friend of my mother's, but she ran off with a bullfighter soon after I was born and we never heard from her again. Cousin Marjorie Brecknock, a great character, simply denied she was my godmother. But King Alfonso, the Duke of Kent, and Aunt Louise, Crown Princess of Sweden, were excellent godparents and I always looked forward to their visits—and when I was very small, their presents. For years I treasured the miniature matadors and bulls that King Alfonso gave me, as well as the gold bracelet with a rather unusual chick-shaped pearl given to me by Prince George, the Duke of Kent.

In 1931, Alfonso, once described by the French newspaper *Le Figaro* as "the happiest and best loved of all the rulers of the earth," had been forced to flee his palace in Madrid, when General Franco's forces seized control in Spain and established the Second Republic. Always one to enjoy splendid surroundings, he chose my parents' sumptuous penthouse in Brook House, overlooking Park Lane, as his place of exile. While my parents had always found the king to be an amusing companion, charming and lively, my father feared that his playboy image and serial adultery would prove his undoing, particularly as he was married to my father's first cousin, Princess Victoria Eugenie of Battenberg. Alfonso always won people over with his charm, however, and my father was no exception, so when he wanted a break from London, the king was welcomed at Adsdean. Brook House and Adsdean were large enough to absorb a king but when my father broke the news of his appointment to the Mediterranean Fleet—and that his house in Malta would be very small—before he could go any farther, Alfonso exclaimed, "Oh, my dear Dickie, how exciting! When do we leave?" So the king went too.

Our most regular visitor was my grandmama. She was accompanied by her devoted lady's maid, Edith Pye—nicknamed by my father many years earlier as "the Pyecrust"— who ensured her "princess" was correctly attired at all times. Handsome and animated, my grandmama always dressed in a white blouse neatly tucked into an ankle-length black skirt.

Her hair was pulled back into a chignon and she wore a fob watch or several gold chains and golden snake rings on her chilblained fingers. She smoked incessantly, using a long glass cigarette holder stuffed with cotton wool to absorb the nicotine, and was rather skillful at taking part in two or three conversations, sometimes in two or three languages, at the same time. She loved a good argument—as my cousin Philip (who would later marry the present queen) used to say, "not just arguments but arguments *about* arguments"—and drew everyone, except my mother, who hated the incessant heated exchanges, into them. She was a tremendous reader, her memory razor sharp, her general knowledge encyclopedic. It helped that she was related to or had met everyone who was anyone in recent history. Nothing was beyond her reach: if her sons were arguing a technical point of naval law, for example, she would break in despite their protestations and say something like, "Well, dear boys, if you look up King's Regulations under Article two fifty-five, clause four, you will find that . . ." And they would look up the reference and discover that she was indeed quite right. She was incredible.

She seldom spoke about the horrors of her past, the ghastly episodes in her life. Her brother Frittie, a hemophiliac, had died when she was ten, after falling from a window; her sister Marie and then her mother died of diphtheria; and later her two sisters Alix (the tsarina) and Ella (the saint) and her Russian nieces and nephew were murdered during the Russian Revolution. When Grandmama wrote to Arthur Balfour, the foreign secretary, to ask whether her nieces, then under house arrest, could come and live with her and her husband on the Isle of Wight, she knew the tsarevitch would not be allowed but hoped the little girls might. But her request was not approved. "The letter breaketh but the spirit maketh alive," she told us, when we asked about her faith.

Even though the king had turned her into a marchioness, she was still a princess in the eyes of her family. My father always kissed her hand before kissing her on the cheek. As children we didn't think much about her royal status, but on one mortifying occasion, after breakfast, Grandmama called my sister over and said, "Patricia, dear child, you know all my *other* granddaughters give me a little curtsy when they say good morning or good night." In point of fact we also kissed her hand and curtsied, but Patricia must have been a bit stiff-kneed that weekend. So rare was it for Grandmama to show any disapproval towards us that ever after my sister's bob was so low she was almost on the floor.

Grandmama smoked a Russian brand of cigarettes called Balkan Sobranie. She kept her glass holder and cigarette case in her petticoat pocket, so would be forever lifting her skirt to get them. She would prod the nicotine-stained cotton wool out of the holder and stick it back in her petticoat, then light another. When she ran out of cigarettes, she groped at her skirt and pointed to my sister or me, saying, "Ah, my dear child . . ." and we would scamper to her room to fetch some more. As I went up the front stairs and along the top to her room, I would hear her coughing and continuing to talk, and coughing and continuing to talk, and by the time I came down again with the cigarettes she was just completing her story. When she decided to cut down, she simply cut the cigarettes in half—which meant we had to go up twice as often to collect the replacements.

Patricia and I would have tea in the billiard room at our own table by the fire. If our parents were at home, they would sit at the other end of the room, drinking tea and conversing

loudly. We would wait patiently for our grandmother to ex-
tricate herself from several arguments, then she would come
over to sit in a chair by the fire as my sister and I huddled
close by on the fire bench to listen. She would then read to
us—usually a chapter of *Alice in Wonderland*—reminding us
succinctly what had gone on before while opening the page
that she had marked with a bay leaf. After a short pause she
would announce the chapter title and the story would begin.
The words were so colorful in our minds because she was
such an amazing mimic: each character was given a different
and sometimes exotic accent, and we would marvel at how
small and polite Alice seemed, and jump with fright as the
duchess roared. When the chapter came to an end, she would
replace the bay leaf and close the book with a smile. We really didn't want her to stop but we didn't dare complain.
Instead we thanked her, said good night, kissed her hand, and
curtsied as we were taken upstairs to bed.

Grandmama's presence at the heart of the family meant
that we often had the pleasure of another visitor, Baroness
Sophie Buxhoeveen. "Isa" had been lady-in-waiting to the
Russian tsarina and had remained with the family when they
were under house arrest during the Revolution. Released by
the Bolsheviks, probably because they thought she was Polish
and they feared an international outcry, she and the family's
foreign tutors remained in Russia, desperately hoping to be
able to help the tsar's family. She explained, her voice always
cracking at this point, how helpless she felt, powerless to do
anything to save them. Eventually, it became clear that if she
wanted to stay alive, she had to flee. I always felt so sad when
she got to the bit in her escape story that involved the tsarevich's little dog Joy, who had escaped into the street and been
rescued by some Czech military officers. They had taken him

with them to Omsk, where by great good fortune he was reunited with Isa. Although the dog was traumatized and by now half-blind, he had barked incessantly, his tail wagging with excitement, at seeing Isa, clearly expecting the tsarevich to appear behind her at any moment. When Isa had to leave, Joy remained by the door for a whole day, pining and crying, and he never did recover his spirits. I used to listen to this story and then go and hug our dogs, telling them how much I loved them, promising they would never suffer the same fate.

After several months, Isa made it to Europe, having traveled across Siberia and east to America. She ultimately settled in England and Grandmama made a little money over to her for being her secretary, although as my grandmother had very little money herself, I suspect it was really my mother who made the allowance. My mother also took care when having her dresses made to have generous hems and large turnings left at the seams so that they could be let out for the impecunious Isa when my mother had finished with them. While Isa looked svelte in the photographs of her younger self at the Russian court, since coming to England she had indulged her sweet tooth and become rather large.

We loved Isa's visits because she had a wonderful sense of self-deprecation, which she needed, as she was always getting into scrapes, having accidents, and generally meeting with bad luck. Her stories were legendary and ridiculous and always had Patricia and me in stitches. My absolute favorite was the one recounting when she had been in the congregation of her Russian Orthodox church and, after praying, she had sat up sharply only to feel loose hair tickling the back of her neck. Quick as a flash she pushed it up into her hat and secured it tightly with a large hairpin. A second or two later, she became aware of a voice very close to her ear whispering, "Madam, would you kindly release my beard." We girls would laugh and clap our hands even though we had heard this story many times before. Grandmama would smile patiently, though not without amusement.

Grandmama and her entourage paid my sister and me a lot of attention, and when I was very young and my parents were away for weeks at a time, my father on naval duties, my mother traveling, I craved their involvement in my games. When I learned to play clock patience, or any new card game, I would ask Grandmama over and over again to play it with me; when Hanky knitted new clothes for my dolls, I would beg the Pyecrust to come and see them; when I felt down in the dumps, I would implore Isa to tell us a story involving one of her disasters. Isa was always most willing to oblige, and in her rich voice would tell us about the time she broke a rib pulling a cracker; how she broke a second rib bending over the arm of a chair to pick up a book; or the time when the hat of the woman next to her burst into flames and she had to jump off the tram, closely followed by a man who landed on top of her, shattering her ankle. Later, at a convent in Rome, where the nuns had spent hours polishing the marble floor in honor of her impending stay, the moment she entered the hall she slipped and broke her leg. She was so good-humored about these mishaps that you didn't feel guilty laughing along with her.

During my early childhood we met lots of my mother's friends, although my sister and I had no indication that some of these friendships ran a little deeper. She was incredibly discreet, and by the time I was five my parents had been practicing their modus vivendi for a number of years. It was about this time that Daddy's friend Yola Letellier started to come and stay. They had met in 1932 at a dance in Deauville, and when my father saw this young, extremely attractive, boyish-looking girl with cropped hair and a little snub nose— a French "gamine"—he wanted to know who she was. *"Ah,"* came the reply. *"Elle est la femme de Letellier."* My father misheard, thinking she was the hotelier's wife, and asked her to dance. In fact Monsieur Letellier was a powerful, much older businessman, whose family owned and ran *Le Journal*, a daily newspaper with the third-highest circulation in the world at that time. Sparks ignited between Yola and my father during that very first dance, and as he whirled her around in a fast Viennese waltz everyone stopped to watch and applaud. Always the showman, my father found this an irresistibly romantic beginning and fell for Yola in a big way. Their relationship was to last for many years, and sometime later the renowned French writer Colette went on to immortalize Yola's story in her novel *Gigi*. In real life, Yola was a free-spirited and youthful as her fictionalized self, though, unlike Gigi, in choosing Henri, Yola had married the older "uncle" and not the young nephew.

My father had learned to accept my mother's boyfriends but my mother found it impossible not to be jealous. The fact that she had been taking lovers for ten years was apparently of no account. When she realized how important Yola was to my father, she cunningly befriended her and took her off to Austria, just at the time my father had arranged precious leave from his ship for their romantic assignation. This must have been extremely galling for my father, but it transpired that my mother's travels with Yola did have one very positive outcome. In 1933, while on some adventure or other, she met a man who changed her life and enabled my father to find some contentment with Yola.

"Bunny" Phillips, or Lieutenant Colonel Harold Phillips

of the Coldstream Guards to give him his proper name, was thrillingly handsome, with perfect posture—rare in a man of six foot five—and being half South American, he rode like a dream. From the moment I first met him, it became impossible to imagine family life without him. He even chose my first pony. Walking on the beach at Bognor, Patricia pointed to a line of little ponies that were giving rides to children. "Isn't that one so sweet," she exclaimed, and Bunny took a good look, patient and interested in what we had to say. While we stopped to have an ice cream, he slipped away to talk to the owner and, a few days later, Sunshine arrived at Adsdean.

We loved having Bunny in our home. Quite simply, he made my mother easier to be around and he genuinely loved being with my sister and me. He had the imagination for wonderful games into which she would also be drawn. When he was away he wrote us warm, affectionate letters, addressing each of us "the Weewaks," one of the many pet names he invented for us. My mother kept many photographs on her dressing table, including the one of my father in naval uniform that she had to frequently replace as he was promoted and decorated. But what never changed was the picture of my mother, Patricia, and me, sitting on a bed in a hotel room in Monte Carlo, all three of us wearing little paper crowns and capes made of the gauzy fabric in which my mother's clothes were packed, grinning dopily at Bunny. This image became the official portrait of the alter egos he invented for us: "Princess Plink" and "Princess Plonk," while he and Mummy were "King and Queen of the Moon." Bunny made up intoxicating stories for our characters, though I always secretly wished I had been the more glamorous-sounding Princess Plink.

Bunny brought great joy to our lives and I loved him deeply. He was a core part of my rather eccentric family, and although he was our mother's lover, they never displayed more than a friendly affection in public. He would stay with us for long periods of time and, to us children, he was just a part of our everyday life. Yola did not live with us but would visit frequently, bringing us charming gifts. For a time, I wouldn't wear anything except the French peasant dress she gave each of us—the pink-and-white-striped skirt, black flowered apron, waistcoat, long ribbons, and little straw hat embroidered with mimosa and worn at a jaunty angle to the side of the head was just about the best thing in the world.

For me, then, the addition of Bunny and Yola and the extension of the family in those two different directions greatly enriched my life and just meant more friendly faces in my somewhat unconventional home. It wasn't until many years later, while riding with my father in the early-morning cool of Delhi, that I realized how his complete lack of jealousy prevented our family from fragmenting and how, as in so many areas of his life, he sought a practical solution to life's tricky problems.

~~ 3 ~~

Casa Medina, our Maltese town house, was built of yellow stone, featured a rather elaborate porch, and much to my delight, had two front doors, each at a different level. It was in Guardamangia, outside Valletta, where the streets were achingly steep and so narrow that if a mule cart or car approached, you had to hop into a doorway to avoid being crushed.

In 1934 my father was still serving in the Mediterranean Fleet and in the summer of that year, Nanny, Miss Vick, Grandmama, Patricia, and I came to spend some time with him. My mother and Bunny joined us later, having returned from a six-month sailing trip around the Pacific. Family life was fun there, full of boat trips and picnics. Daddy was in a particularly happy mood, sharing memories of his own childhood days in Malta when my grandfather was commander in chief of the Mediterranean Fleet. We explored the island with him and he showed us the beautiful blue lagoons where we could swim, and he gave me a donkey to ride. My sister and I were also given a chameleon each. I named mine Casper and could watch him for ages, endlessly fascinated as to how he changed from yellow to dark green. He spent hours balanced on my hand, his long tongue darting out to catch flies, his eyes revolving in different directions.

Peter Murphy and Noël Coward came to stay, making my parents laugh as they competed with each other to tell the funniest anecdotes. As an officer's wife, my mother was responsible for hosting a cocktail party. This was nonnegotiable. The only day when she could possibly fulfill this duty, however, was a Sunday, which was the only day on which a party was not supposed to happen. Peter and Noël encouraged her to send out the invitations anyway. Noël was there when the replies arrived, including one that read, "Lieutenant Wood thanks Lady Louis Mountbatten for her invitation but would rather not accept on a Sunday." During the party— held on a Sunday—my mother was puzzled by a long queue forming outside the gentlemen's cloakroom. When the guests left, she darted in to see what had been keeping them in there for so long. Stuck up above the cistern, she found a piece of paper in Noël's handwriting:

> *Lieutenant Wood is never bored*
> *On days devoted to the Lord*
> *In fact he thinks himself as one*
> *With God the Father, God the Son*
> *And, though he'd rather die than boast*
> *Also with God the Holy Ghost*

At the end of the summer Mummy and Bunny left for a long holiday. Patricia and I remained in Malta, collecting the stamps and postcards they sent from Bangkok, Angkor Wat, Hawaii, Bali, Java, Suva, Borneo, Sarawak, Bangkok (again), Calcutta, Jodhpur, Baghdad, Cairo, and Budapest. A little later we had to return to England because our father was appointed to his first command, in charge of sailing a new destroyer to Singapore, which he was ordered to exchange for an older ship. He wrote on the return journey informing us of a rather surprising package that my mother and Bunny had left for him to collect in Hong Kong—a black Malayan honey bear named Rastus. When Patricia and I returned to Malta to see Daddy the following year, I was not at all pleased to make Rastus's acquaintance. When he reared up on his hind legs he was as tall as my six-year-old self. To tell the truth, I was frightened of him; when we met in the garden I would run away, but that didn't help as he delighted in chasing me. Actually everyone was slightly scared of him, with the natural exception of Grandmama. Until her arrival, Rastus had been enjoying free rein and was not very biddable, but he soon had a run-in with our grandmother. One teatime she discovered him on the table eating all the cakes. "Down, sir," she cried in outrage. "Get down at once!" Rastus of course got down at once. There was no one—human or animal—who could not be put in their place by Grandmama.

When Yola arrived she brought with her a funny little short-haired dachshund puppy with slightly googly eyes. "Ah, ma petite Pamela," she called, "voici un petit cadeau." Yola spoke very little English and we were usually required to speak to her in French. "Do you like?" she added, because I had gone very silent. I couldn't find the words to express myself in any language. It was more than "like"—it was love at first sight. "Elle s'appelle Lottie—après Lottie Minkus," she continued, and although I had never heard of the opera singer then, it sounded like the perfect name for such a darling companion. I picked up my puppy and cuddled her, only to be told by Nanny that I couldn't play with her until I had written Yola a thank-you note. I spent the afternoon in a fug of despair, writing out in French *"Merci . . . beaucoup . . . pour . . . le . . . petit . . . chien"* in a painstakingly careful hand because I knew that if I made a mistake I would have to start all over again. All I wanted to do was play with my puppy, and as I pressed my pencil harder and harder into the paper, my hand hurting with the effort, I felt a bitter resentment well up inside me.

That summer Lottie became the center of my life and I, in return, became the object of her love. She faithfully trotted after me wherever we went and I looked after her as if my life depended on it. Everything went smoothly until one hot, heart-stopping day when we all went out in a little green motor yacht so that my father could indulge in his new obsession. Waterskiing was a comparatively new sport in the thirties but my father was already hooked. He had been driving along La Croisette in Cannes a few years earlier when he saw a man "with two long wooden planks attached to his feet." He was so impressed that he sought the man out, bought the ski kit from him, and soon became an excellent skier. On more than one occasion, when his ship had stopped at sea, he skied out to dinner between ships in full mess dress with trousers rolled up and shoes hanging by their laces around his neck, effortlessly dropping the ski rope when he reached the ladder of the other ship. On this day in Malta, as my mother and Yola lay chatting and sunbathing, I walked around the boat to watch my father ski, something I always found mesmerizing, like flying across the water. Lottie was following me along the narrow edge of the boat when it suddenly lurched; she lost her footing and dropped into the waves. The world seemed to stop turning and I screamed at the top of my voice. My father simply skied by, scooped Lottie up, and placed her back on board.

This blissful summer of 1935 was cut short by Mussolini's ferocious expansion of his empire as he prepared to invade Abyssinia, which shared a border with the Italian colony of Eritrea. In the climate of growing aggression, it was decided that all naval families should leave the Mediterranean. For my parents, this was a problem, as they had been expecting to stay in Malta for two or three years: Adsdean was let and Brook House was uninhabitable, in the midst of major renovations. Believing the crisis would be over within a couple of months, my parents decided that Patricia, I, Nanny, Miss Vick—and mercifully Lottie—should go to Budapest until the situation calmed down. Mummy and Bunny went on ahead in the Hispano, while the rest of us traveled by train. We broke the journey at an island in the Danube, a relief for Patricia and me, as the atmosphere in the carriage was decidedly icy. Circumstances had forced our two guardians at least to pretend to get on but the underlying frostiness between them made my sister and me uncomfortable. The hotel soon made up for it, though, as it had a swimming pool with a machine that made enormous waves every few minutes. A bell was rung beforehand to warn vulnerable swimmers to scramble out so that the waves could start. We hadn't understood the warning and I was nearly drowned as the waves crashed over my head. There was hardly any time to catch my breath before another mountain of waves rose up in front of me, but luckily Nanny was there to pull me out of the danger zone.

Reunited with my mother and Bunny, we continued onwards until we found a small hotel in the mountains about two hours east of Budapest. Kekes Szallo was hidden in a pine forest, and once our mother decided it would do, she settled us in, gave my sister and me a quick kiss, and got back in the Hispano with Bunny, leaving the four of us—and Lottie—while they continued on their travels.

At first, the freedom of Kekes was exhilarating. Patricia and I had hardly ever been together for such a sustained period of time and now we were never apart. At eleven years old, she was going through a writing phase and, rather thrillingly, created lots of scary stories for me about a stag. Something in the mountain air—or maybe because there was no alternative—seemed to put a halt to the hostilities between Nanny and Miss Vick, and the four of us enjoyed ourselves enormously. Each day we walked bravely through the mountain forests, only a little bit scared we would encounter the wolves we had been told lurked among the trees. My sister and I wore the same thing for every walk—little cotton dresses, white gym shoes, and white ankle socks—and carried rucksacks on our backs. As we walked, we learned to lean on the sticks that had been specially cut down for the purpose of hiking. Lottie was in heaven—running in and out of the trees and helping collect the twigs for the wigwams we made as we picnicked at the local First World War memorial. In the evening we ate at the hotel—a lot of ham, I seem to remember.

The Abyssinian crisis went on and on and no one came to get us. We had left Malta in July with only our summer clothes, so by October, when Mussolini's troops attacked Abyssinia, it was cold and beginning to snow in the Hungarian mountains. In the local village Miss Vick and Nanny bought us all matching pink flannel underwear and a few winter outer clothes, so at least we could go tobogganing. Heaven knows where they found the money to do so because our funds were running perilously short. When the manager informed Miss Vick that the hotel would be providing a limited service

during the winter, she and Nanny—united by their panic—
sent frantic messages to Malta. But communication was difficult and no answers or help came. By the time the manager
insisted that we settle our bill, we had run out of money. It
was a stroke of luck that Dr. Toth, a guest at the same time
as us, overheard the kerfuffle, assured the manager that our
mother was a famous and rich English aristocrat, and guar-
anteed the money. Such a kind act by a complete stranger was
a godsend and ensured we still had a roof over our heads.

By the end of October we still hadn't received any word
from our parents, but finally, one snowy day, we awoke to
find my mother and Yola in reception. Apparently, my mother
had written down the name of the hotel on a piece of paper
then lost it. In early November she decided that she and Yola
had better retrace the route she had driven earlier in the year
and so it was that, at last, we were found, rescued, and all
bills were settled. Dr. Toth had left by this time, so my mother
was unable to thank him, though many years later, towards
the end of the 1960s, when he was in a Siberian labor camp,
he wrote and asked me for some help. He had enclosed a list
of food available from the Soviet store GUM, which was the
only source permitted. I immediately ordered as much as he
was allowed. Sadly I never heard back from him and fear he
must have died in the camp.

We couldn't return to England, as our houses were still
unavailable, so our father arranged for us to go and stay with
our great-aunt and -uncle, in Darmstadt, Germany. As reign-
ing Grand Duke of Hesse and a passionate aesthete, Uncle
Ernie had created an artists' colony at Darmstadt, attracting
leading architects and artists from all over the world. The
city's skyline was dominated, as it is today, by a forty-eight-
meter-high art deco "Wedding Tower" that had been erected

to celebrate Uncle Ernie's second marriage, to Aunt Onor. My mother drove us down there, settled us in, and then went back to Malta to pack up her things so that she could go traveling in China. It wasn't safe for us to be in Malta, and my father, disappointed not to have us back with him, wrote long letters to compensate.

Patricia and I were very happy in Darmstadt, even though I was sick for a while with a bad case of measles. We lived right in the center of town in the magnificently large Neues Palais, which had been built in 1865 for Princess Alice, Queen Victoria's daughter, when she married Uncle Ernie's father. My great-aunt Onor was extremely kind and patient, teaching me how to knit and, when I became frustrated at my lack of progress, encouraging me by hiding in the ball of wool tiny wooden toys that fell out as it unwound. Old Uncle Ernie drew me the same fanciful drawings of monsters that he had drawn for my father when he was a child. He called them "katoofs" and I was thrilled in my turn to have them drawn for me. We also learned to speak German while we were there and Patricia's letters greatly impressed my father—it became quite obvious that she now spoke the language better than he did. I discovered only after we left, however, that the thick Hessian accent I had picked up from the servants meant that my German was pretty useless anywhere else.

It was strange to be away from our parents that Christmas but myriad cousins from all over Europe kept us busy and on our toes, and waking each morning, we never quite knew which language we were going to need. Mummy and Bunny were still sending us postcards. They traveled through China, by the Trans-Siberian railway, through the Philippines, Celebes, and Moluccas, then on to Bali, Java, Hong Kong, and Japan, where they finally turned for home via California. We collected the stamps and Nanny made an album for me to fill with our pictures from Kekes and Mummy's postcards. Poor Daddy spent Christmas Day alone in Malta, his meal leftovers from the staff lunch.

At New Year, 1936, we heard the grown-ups talking sadly about the death of King George V. Somehow, England seemed so far away and I was both distracted and charmed by my new surroundings. We loved to drive out to Uncle Ernie's charming property, Wolfsgarten, and to his hunting boxes and farms, especially as I was allowed to perch up beside the coachman as he drove Max and Mauritz, a pair of the most magnificent carriage horses. At the farms we were given warm milk to drink straight from the cows—a sweet taste and a creamy texture so different to the horrible goat's milk that I was used to drinking in Malta. My sister and I enjoyed playing in a tiny white house in the grounds of Wolfsgarten, though its history made us tremendously sad. Uncle Ernie had built it as a surprise for his much-loved and only child, Elizabeth, after she had described to him the little house of her dreams: hidden in the woods, with white walls, a steep roof, a chimney looped to look like a needle, and glass witch balls in the garden to keep her safe. A year later, on her seventh birthday, he had presented her with the house, with an inscription carved over the door: "This little house was built just for me in the year 1902." Tragically the witch balls did not keep her safe, for she died later that same year, from typhoid. The story made me shiver, and secretly I was a bit apprehensive about playing in the house, as I was soon to turn the same age as Elizabeth was when she died.

Patricia and I came back to England in the late spring of 1936. My father had now been appointed to the Admiralty, the house in Malta had been packed up for the foreseeable future, and my mother stopped traveling and returned to Adsdean. It felt so good to be back under the same roof as my parents and Bunny; to be reunited with Hanky, our ponies, and our childhood things. It had been strangely dislocating to be away for so long, and while I had seen so many new places, lived with and become fond of kindly relatives, I was happiest in my own home.

## 4

Patricia and I had been away for almost a year, so at first it was a novelty being back in Adsdean. I noticed things in a different way—the stunning view from the tower rooms; my father's handwritten fire instructions lining the corridors that included a role for the coxswain (baffling until Patricia explained he must have copied out the drill from his ship's emergency procedures); the colorful bunches of flowers that adorned every room; and, of course, our much-missed horses and ponies. My sister and I had become even more horse mad, and that spring of 1936 was full of our "Adsdean gym-khanas," as well as horse-themed games around the house.

It took a bit of getting used to being back with my mother, especially when Bunny wasn't around. She was very prickly, and we all had to be very careful of what we said in her company. Sometimes it was as if we were treading on eggshells— she would be hurt by the most unlikely things and then sulk for hours afterwards. In contrast you could say anything you liked to my father, and I adored sharing a house with him once more. He was so inventive, constantly thinking up things that would make Patricia and me happy. That Easter Sunday, he told us to stay up in the nursery. When the call came, we rushed down to the narrow walled garden. The long green carpet of lawn was studded with brightly colored papier-mâché eggs adorned with pictures of Easter bunnies and chicks. Some of the eggs were huge, and we ran around gathering them in our arms and then carefully opening each one, with cries of delight at the surprises they contained.

But it was when we went riding with my father that I felt most alive and free. I relished the days when we all went out together, riding up into the Downs, a journey of about half an hour to the northeast of the house. We trotted in single file through the narrow lane known as Nut Walk, the horses' hooves crushing the chalky stones of the path, then climbed a steep track lined with hazel bushes. A bit farther up, the bracken grew so tall—taller even than my pony's ears—that my father called it "elephant grass," after which we turned off to the right and cantered up to the South Downs. Here the landscape was bare and wild except for the broom and clumps of yew and gorse. When the broom was in bloom its scent filled the air, a sure sign that spring was coming. We would gallop across the Downs, ignoring warnings to "watch those rabbit holes!"

As spring took hold of the countryside and the acrid smell of wild garlic filled the air, my sister and I picked primroses and bee orchids for the table in the day nursery. Grandmama could name every tree and flower but I was still pretty hopeless—though not for want of being told. Always busy inventing something or other, my father had recently created a nine-hole golf course in the park. He had installed a clubhouse and employed a "pro" who could give guests a lesson. My sister and I didn't play but my mother was surprisingly good. I tried a couple of times but I couldn't understand, having all that wild countryside around us, why anybody would want to hit a ball around such a limited bit of land.

My father was a master at solving problems. When I lied about taking some chocolate and, as I vehemently denied it, puffed chocolate fumes into Nanny's face, she was cross. "This is very serious indeed, Pammy. Wait until Daddy comes home." To me this sounded like a death sentence, and when she added, "I am not going to punish you, we will wait until we tell Daddy and see what he says," I knew I was done for. My father was not due to come home for several days and each hour of waiting was agony. I couldn't sleep and Nanny maintained a severe expression whenever she looked my way. When my father finally sent for me—a relief in some ways, at least the waiting was over—I braced myself. "Nanny tells me that you took a piece of chocolate." He spoke in a quiet, reasonable voice. "That was naughty, Pammy. But what has really upset her very much is that you told a lie. It's very important in life that you don't tell lies. And so you understand why, I am going to tell you a story about a nun." I was surprised at the way this conversation was going. "Now nuns are good people. They would never do an evil thing and the nun in this story had never ever told a lie. But there came a moment during a war between the Catholics and the Protestants when she was asked to hide a Protestant man. Of course, this nun was a Catholic. When the soldiers came into the convent, they asked her, 'Has a Protestant man been here asking you to hide him?' Looking them straight in the eye she replied, 'No.' She lied because she knew that the soldiers would kill the man if they found him. And because she was a nun, and nuns are always truthful, the soldiers believed her and went away." He paused so the story could sink in. I was only seven, so probably looked a little blank. My father took me by the shoulders and said, gently, "You see, Pammy darling, you probably only have one, *maybe* two opportunities in the whole of your life to tell a lie. So don't waste them on chocolate." The message went in, all the more so because he hadn't scolded me but had told me a story that I could think about. It stayed with me for a very long time and made me very sorry for having lied about something so trivial.

In the summer of 1936, King Edward VIII came to Adsdean with Mr. and Mrs. Simpson. I was excited about the king coming to our house and looking forward to making my deep curtsy to him. During the afternoon following their arrival Hanky came up to the nursery to share the news that Mrs. Simpson had "presented her ladyship with a cold cooked chicken from Fortnum's" and our chef, Mr. Brinz, was in a tizzy about what to do with it, when there were so many to be fed and he was well prepared. Mr. Brinz was not to be crossed. Once my mother had told him that if the cake he always offered alongside dessert remained untouched, then it could be kept for the next day. Mr. Brinz had said nothing but the next day, at the bottom of his legendary copperplate menu, was written *Le gâteau d'hier.*

After Mr. Simpson left the next morning, Mrs. Simpson and the king remained and there was a good deal of talking among the adults. Towards the end of that year the king gave up his throne so that he could marry Wallis Simpson and this caused a huge crisis. I was surprised to learn that my cousin Lilibet and her sister Margaret Rose would actually have to live in Buckingham Palace and that, eventually, Lilibet would be queen. This took some digesting.

Now that Patricia had turned twelve, she was sent to school in London, returning home on the weekends. During the week I spent hours playing alone, paddling down the long corridors in our model four-wheeled canoe or pulling Lottie in the little German wagon we had brought back from

Darmstadt. I came out of my imaginary world when I heard the horses being brought round to the mounting block: riding made me feel real and happy. But this was not a good time for me. Miss Vick had left when Patricia started school, to be replaced by Mademoiselle Chevrier, whom we immediately christened Zelle. And then Nanny left too. I heard adults muttering that this was "a good thing" as she had become a "little too possessive" of me, but I was not at all happy. I was puzzled by Miss Crichton Miller, who came to look after me and begin preparing me for school. She kept asking me a lot of questions and she watched me play in a different way to Nanny. I didn't know what "highly strung" or "not particularly sociable" meant, but they didn't sound very good. She did take me to see the deer in Cowdray Park, however, and was nice in a remote sort of way, completely unlike my much-adored Nanny.

If Mummy was at home, then that meant Bunny would be there too, but they never stayed for very long. During the winter of 1937, the postcards began to roll in again, showing the animals they had seen in Kenya, Uganda, and the Belgian Congo. I stuck the cards in an album but it didn't really make up for their not being around. I cheered up a lot when I was told that my mother was coming home for my eighth birthday, especially when the news of her return from Africa was delivered with an air of mystery and none of us could quite work out what was going on. My father left for the airport with no idea what he would discover, and was amazed to see her descend from the plane with a three-month-old lion cub in her arms. "His name is Sabi," she told him. "His mother was shot in the Transvaal for attacking a man and poaching cattle. We simply had to bring him back with us." It had been easy enough to get the lion cub on a plane in Africa. There was a momentary hiccup, however, when she and Bunny disembarked in London and the airport authorities told them that Sabi needed to go into quarantine, as they couldn't think where. My father—suppressing his shock at my mother's cargo—reassured the authorities that Adsdean could become an official site for lion quarantine and all was fixed. By now a seasoned traveler, Sabi settled down on the parcel shelf of the car and was driven to our house by my astonished father.

Sabi was adorable and became a treasured member of our menagerie. He was as small as the Sealyham terriers and it amused me to watch guests' surprise as they bumped into him outside while he was having a tussle with one of the dogs over a towel or a toy. He loved the golf course and would lie sunning himself in the sandy bunkers, although he did unfortunately also like to use them as litter trays. He also enjoyed lying in wait on the high banks around the croquet lawn, when Grandmama and her friend Mrs. Jenkins were playing, gathering himself up, then suddenly propelling himself from his hiding place and charging down towards the old ladies, scattering the croquet balls everywhere. When we had lunch he would lie under the dining room table and chew any available walking stick belonging to an elderly relative. He grew so fast that he was soon much bigger than the dogs, and although he never bit or clawed, he was so strong that he knocked me over a couple of times. When he started to get up on his hind legs and rest his paws on people's shoulders, he was quickly rehoused in a loose box in the stables.

My mother had returned from her travels in time to commission a dress—she chose a glamorous, slinky column of silver sequins—for King George VI's coronation. I too had a new dress made—long, white with silver threads, a little posy of artificial flowers and green ribbons at the waist—and most thrillingly of all, a vibrant apple-green velvet cloak with a pale-green velvet lining. Being so young, on the actual day of the coronation I was left behind at Buckingham Palace while my mother and sister went to Westminster Abbey. I didn't mind—it was such fun to watch the procession and I felt a stab of pride as I caught sight of my father riding just behind the king and queen's splendid gold coach amid the dancing flags and cheering crowds.

Old Brook House had been sold to a developer while we were in Malta and my mother had since bought the two-story penthouse that would take its place. This is where Patricia and Zelle now lived during the week, and sometimes I would be taken in the staff bus from Adsdean to visit the family there. The views over Hyde Park were spectacular, and in the summer, when the trees were in leaf, all you could see from the back of the house was greenery and the odd church spire. It was difficult to tell that you were in London. The new Brook House was much more contained than Adsdean and I especially liked the huge Van Dyck portraits that hung in the long hallway. I could instantly recognize a Tudor or a Stuart—much faster than I could recognize a relation—and as I skipped past, I would say a cheerful "Good morning!" to each one, stories about their lives running through my mind. I also loved examining the stunning trompe l'oeil panels, newly painted—in a soft pale grayish blue—by the artist Rex Whistler. There were fanciful depictions of the countries my mother had visited; images of the family houses; armorials with naval, music, and gardening themes; and a portrait of Sabi playing with a snake.

By this stage, in autumn 1937, it was my turn to go to school—Buckswood Grange, near Crawley. I was eight and a half, and after leading such a quiet life at home without Patricia, being away at boarding school was unnervingly chaotic. My life thus far had been comparatively calm—sometimes the only person I would talk to all day was Nanny—so the constant and endless noise of school was horrifying. I just couldn't find any peace among the clamor of the everyday: the din at mealtimes; the scraping of chairs and banging of doors; the playground awash with running, screaming girls; and the giggling at night as soon as the dorm lights went out. I felt very miserable. Eventually, on the advice of a doctor, the school did something about my discomfort and I was allowed to spend leisure time alone. I would take a book and find an undisturbed corner in which to read, while the other girls played their frenetic games.

It wasn't that I didn't have good friends at school. I did. But I preferred playing with one girl rather than in a big group. Belinda was a perfect choice—quiet, rather serious, and like me, highly conscientious when it came to schoolwork. Belinda's parents were tea planters in India, and when her mother came to England, she would often take Belinda and me out to tea. On one such occasion, she suggested we might like to go with her to the polo at Cowdray Park. I could hardly contain my delight when I discovered that my father was playing in the second match, skipping over to kiss him at the end of the chukka. He was even more astonished, and then rather embarrassed, that somebody else was taking me out for tea when he was close to the school.

My mother did come to take tea at school and I invited Belinda along. I remember that on one occasion, Miss Fairburns, our headmistress, offered around a plate of scones and my mother, midstory, took one but held it aloft in her small, perfectly manicured hand, gesticulating occasionally as she finished her anecdote. When it was over she smiled at Miss Fairburns's appreciative comments and then popped the little scone into her mouth. Belinda, who could be terribly serious, could not contain herself: "Oh, but Lady Louis, at Buckswood we always put our food on our plate *before* we eat!" I couldn't have been more surprised and glanced anxiously from Mummy to Miss Fairburns and back to Belinda, who was looking characteristically unmoved. Poor Miss Fairburns, appearing not a little flushed, said, "Belinda! You must apologize to Lady Louis this instant!" Luckily, my mother was always sweetness itself to my friends: "No, no, Miss Fairburns, please don't worry, Belinda is quite right. Where *are* my manners?" And she turned the conversation effortlessly and immediately to the less controversial topic of the school's roses.

Miss Fairburns shared the running of the school with her partner, "the other headmistress," Miss Haines. She only ever dressed in a brown suit, shirt, and tie and she was as pointy as Miss Fairburns was soft and billowy. I was very fond of Miss Fairburns but was mortified when my parents asked her and Miss Haines to lunch at Adsdean. My father was apt to become lost in thought as he plotted a new signaling maneuver or some such thing. On this occasion, the two principals were seated on the other side of the table to my father and to my alarm I noticed that he was sitting in silence and had begun to roll up little pellets of bread that he began to flick towards his glass so that they pinged back towards him. Suddenly one ricocheted over Miss Fairburns's plate. My father didn't notice but she stiffened in alarm and throughout the rest of the meal she and Miss Haines remained visibly jumpy. I was able to relax only when my mother finally rang for coffee and my father awoke from his reverie. He seemed oblivious to the dozens of little bread balls scattered in front of him. I wished Belinda had been there to tell him off.

Belinda wasn't always serious, though, and together we prone to fits of giggles and madcap schemes, such as the occasion during my second year when we decided it was high time that all the girls in our dormitory ran away. We plotted in hushed tones at lunch and tea and spent the whole of the next week stuffing our elasticated knickers with bread rolls. On the appointed evening we went to bed as good as gold— no doubt alerting the teachers straightaway that something was amiss—and at the prearranged hour, we dressed furtively, then sneaked out one by one into the corridor. But I was paralyzed by a sudden thought: who would look after Sunshine if I didn't go back home? As a special treat Sunshine had been allowed to come with me to school and was housed at the local stables. "Come on, Pammy," hissed Belinda, "what are you waiting for?" She gave me a shove. "I can't come," I said, "I can't leave Sunshine." "Don't be such a chump," she replied, pulling me along. But what did she know? She didn't have a pony and couldn't possibly understand. I shook myself free, handed over my bread rolls, then went back to bed, feeling like the worst traitor ever. It wasn't long before the other girls came back too: they had made it as far as the roof before they were caught and sent straight back to bed.

At Adsdean, my family was coming to terms with two recent tragedies. The first involved some of my German cousins. Cecile, my cousin Philip's older sister, was married to Don, Uncle Ernie's son, and they had three children with another on the way. Cecile had been so kind in Germany, when we were living with Aunt Onor and Uncle Ernie, even writing to me in England, inquiring as to the health of one of my dolls. I was looking forward to seeing them again at the wedding of Don's brother Lu Hesse to Peg Geddes. The Hessian family— including Aunt Onor (Uncle Ernie had recently died)—was

traveling to London, and there was a great sense of antici-
pation with all the family coming together. They set off by
plane from Germany but in thick fog they crashed into a
brickworks' chimney in Ostend and everyone on board was
killed. Cecile's little girl, Johanna, had been left in Germany
as she was too young to come to the wedding, and I couldn't
stop thinking of her now all alone, without her parents or
her brothers or her grandmother.

Then, one afternoon as I was going into the drawing
room, Patricia said, "Don't go in there just now, Pammy. It's
Grandmama. She is writing a letter"—she paused, realizing
she hadn't given me enough of an explanation—"and she's
crying." There was nothing I could say after the shock of this
revelation, so I went into the garden to play with Lottie. I had
never seen a grown-up cry before and I didn't like the feeling it gave me. I knew why she was in tears, for her son, my
father's brother Georgie, had died from cancer that spring,
just before my birthday. There seemed to be all sorts of bad
news around, and at that time the grown-ups never seemed
to be totally free of worries. Knowing that our grandmother,
usually so strong and resilient, was in tears made me very
unhappy.

Maybe you couldn't be sure of the world after all. There
was talk of war too, a rumbling undercurrent of unease that
ran through the snatches of conversation I overheard between my parents, Bunny, and their guests. Too young for
anyone to explain the facts to me, I was unsettled, as if I
didn't know what I would wake up to the next morning. I
didn't like this feeling one bit.

## 5

Ever since the beginning of 1938, my mother had been heavily involved with the nation's preparations for the war that seemed increasingly inevitable. She joined the Red Cross and attended first-aid and antigas demonstrations and accompanied the king and queen to air-raid precaution lectures in London. Most local boroughs had started to stockpile gas masks and conduct public air-raid demonstrations. My father secured masks for everyone at Adsdean and carried out his own drills. In the park below the terrace where we all assembled, gas masks covering our faces, the danger of an attack seemed far away. In London, the atmosphere was much more tense.

For me, at school or at home, the signs of the impending crisis were few and far between. That summer, Cousin Philip often came over to stay, which was always good fun. He was my first cousin, the son of my father's sister, Princess Alice of Greece. Eight years older than me and three years Patricia's senior, he was the inspiration behind all the naughty, boisterous games we played, including vicious bicycle polo matches with my father. Philip was very handsome, and even though he was my cousin, hero worship blossomed during those innocent months. I was in awe of him.

It was in September that pictures of the prime minister, Neville Chamberlain—the peace settlement in one hand and his black umbrella in the other—appeared all over the newspapers. The house was alive with adults discussing the newspaper headline "Peace in Our Time." I had to catch Patricia one day to ask her what it all meant. She explained that the prime minister had gone to Germany to have a meeting with their leader, Adolf Hitler, who said that, after the horrors of the First World War, he didn't want to go to war with us. That sounded good to me, so I was confused as to why my parents were cross with the prime minister and kept telling everyone that they were "antiappeasement." In fact one day at tea, when Zelle casually mentioned that she had been stopped in the street by someone collecting for "appeasement" and, having been persuaded that it was a good national cause, had given him quite a bit of money, my mother cried, "No, Zelle! That won't do any good at all." I listened then as my father patiently explained why they believed appeasement was wrong, thinking that Hitler could not be trusted.

There followed another extended period when my parents were both away—my father on naval duties and my mother on a challenging adventure with Bunny along the newly completed Burma Road to China. She wrote to tell us how her presence had astonished the Chinese officials, as she was the first woman to travel along the road. Apart from the fact that she could never find a woman's toilet, she didn't encounter any problems along the way, even though there were hostilities between the Chinese and the Japanese at the time. In May 1939—she missed my tenth birthday—she came home with two wallabies, Dabo and Bobo, a gift from New Guinea. When my mother had asked what she should feed them, she had been told, "Oh! Too easy, too easy. Just give them orchids and they will be fine." Eventually it was established what alternatives would suit them if orchids were found not to be abundant in England.

In the summer of 1939, as war rapidly became a certainty, my mother volunteered to take in some evacuees. Her father had recently died, bequeathing Broadlands to her, but as there were more important matters at hand, and many of our staff had been conscripted, my parents decided we should remain at Adsdean for a while. In August, twenty-four children and two teachers came down from Wimbledon. They arrived looking completely underdressed for a large, cold country house, shivering away in their skimpy cotton dresses and short trousers. Rationing was beginning to test even the magical powers of Mr. Brinz, but these children melted his heart. As they were from London, he decided that fish and chips would be the most familiar food and he dished them up a large quantity for their first tea with us. The children looked at their plates in great confusion, then looked at each other, looked at their teachers, and promptly declared the feast inedible without vinegar or newspaper.

On 3 September, my sister and I were sent for. As we came down from the nursery to join our parents, we could sense by the stillness in the house that something of great significance was happening. We sat in silence, listening to the declaration of war as Mr. Chamberlain's bleak voice was relayed from the wireless. I had never heard an announcement on the radio before and I lay in bed that night wondering what it would be like to wake up in the morning "at war." The next day, however, nothing had changed, and after a few more days my father came back from HMS *Kelly* at Portsmouth and took Patricia, Grandmama, and me for a picnic lunch at Maiden Castle in Dorset. Scrambling up the tremendous grass mounds at the castle and looking down at the undulating fields and forests below, I felt like a medieval knight looking out for invaders.

I had now inherited Patricia's pony Puck, who was bigger than Sunshine. One morning my father was waiting to be recalled to the *Kelly*. As he knew that he was due to go to sea at any moment, he wanted to enjoy a last ride, so he decided to take Patricia and me in turn, leaving the other to stay close to the telephone and act as a "dispatch rider." It sounded rather thrilling. During Patricia's ride I had never prayed so much for something to happen, and after watching the phone for what seemed like ages, I went to the stables to make sure that Puck was tacked up, ready for the off. When I heard our butler, Frank Randall, telling Mr. Birch, the head groom, in an urgent voice, "You must saddle up and ride out to find his lordship," my heart began to pound. "But Mr. Randall," said Birch, "his lordship has left strict instructions that Miss Pamela should act as the courier." "Oh, I don't think we can have Miss Pamela going up there on that little pony. No, Mr. Birch, you will have to go." Horrified that the moment might be denied me, I cried, "No, no, Frank. Daddy wants me to go, that's why they left me here." I ran past him, leapt onto Puck, and careered away before he could stop me. It took quite a while to catch up with my father and Patricia, and Puck—who was gone in the wind—was making a lot of noise by the time we reached them. I could hardly speak with excitement: "Daddy, the telephone call has come. You've got to go back to your ship!" Knowing that I had done something important all by myself made me feel giddy with triumph. As my father and Patricia galloped off, Puck and I stood together in a cloud of dust, wheezing and puffing for a while, until I collected the reins and we turned for home.

This was the last time I was to gallop across this stretch of the Downs, for while I was at school that autumn, my parents left Adsdean and moved to Broadlands. When I came home for the half-term holidays, I was astonished to discover that my new house was a proper stately home, set among six thousand acres of land. Despite the beauty of the inside of the house, it was the outside that captured my imagination. The River Test flowed by below the front lawn and through the magical gardens that had been shaped by Capability Brown for the first Viscount Palmerston in the eighteenth century. Mr. Brown had constructed an ornamental canal along which there were some spectacular features, including the ornamental dairy, designed for the delight of the Palmerston ladies and their guests. Here, like Marie Antoinette, they could play at milking and butter making. When I discovered it for the first time I was enthralled—it was like entering a museum with all the old churns, large china bowls, and wooden spoons lying around, and as I picked them all up, I felt as though I were being transported back in time.

From the dairy you had a choice of where to go next. You could either return to the house by following the canal that disappeared by the old icehouse into a tunnel below the lawn, reemerging beyond the house to run through the pleasure grounds and finally join the river. Or you could turn left up one of a flight of paired stone steps through some decorative gates and into the walled gardens. The steps met at the top in a wide stone plinth upon which my grandfather had carved on the left-hand side "Lest We Forget. The Great War 1914–1918." The right-hand side was empty, and six years later my father was sorely tempted to have carved "As We Forgot. Second World War 1939–1945." There were three gardens enclosed by the wall. The first had apple tunnels on two sides and a greenhouse, and the walls themselves were covered in espaliered plum trees. Here too was a pool with mulberry trees planted by King James I. The next was a flower and vegetable garden and, farther on still, a section that had once been my stepgrandmother Molly's white garden. Beyond and below all three was a tranquil Japanese garden with a decorative bridge and a summerhouse over a pool. I loved the large bronze sculptures of a stork and a heron that stood in the water.

I was particularly enamored of the glass orangery in which grew orange and lemon trees, reminding me of Malta, as well as camellia and gardenia. The third Lord Palmerston, Queen Victoria's prime minister, had held parliamentary meetings in it nearly one hundred years before. It was quite awe inspiring and I felt strangely honored to be there. Lottie and I ran around, discovering parts of the house and gardens, for a week—though there were times when I panicked, overwhelmed by the sheer scale of everything, worried I might become lost in all the space or swallowed up by the high clipped hedges. My father was away with the *Kelly*, Bunny with the Coldstream Guards, and although my mother had finally been able to volunteer her services, she had yet to find a position that could fill up her time and employ her ample amounts of energy and drive. When we weren't at school, she, Patricia, and I rattled around the large house with the dogs. My sister and I expected things to be very low-key for Guy Fawkes Night because fireworks were banned, but our mother surprised us by taking us down to the cellars and letting off indoor fireworks, allowing us to run about giggling and waving sparklers in the dark, underground passages. When it was time to go back to school—Buckswood had been evacuated to Rhyl in North Wales as a safety precaution—I still hadn't explored the house fully.

A lot of knitting went on that winter. My mother was given duties in the depot for knitted garments for the Royal Navy and at school we spent a great deal of time knitting for the brave soldiers, sailors, and airmen who were risking their lives for us. Actually I felt terribly sorry for them—for being away from home, in danger, and also for having to wear the garments we made for them. I couldn't believe anyone would actually wear the scarves, socks, and balaclava helmets we were producing. But it wasn't only at the depot that my mother worked—she had also joined the Joint War Organisation of the Red Cross and St. John Ambulance— and it seemed that all this work was changing her. There was a bounce in her step, she loved planning and organizing and making things happen, and she had the skills, charm, and presence to make a difference, propelling her towards every opportunity that came her way. She looked dashing in her uniform and cap, forever set at a jaunty angle. Our new Brook House had been bombed, so the family's London base was now a small house in Charles Street, Mayfair. The depot my mother was supervising was in Belgravia, so it meant that she could walk between the two in a brisk fifteen minutes. She had to call in the help of as many people as she could, including Zelle and Isa, and I couldn't help worrying that accident-prone Isa might fall foul of some knitting needles.

I noticed my father looking at my mother with a new sense of pride, telling us that she had found her "purpose in life." He, on the other hand, was a bit down. *Kelly* was making only short forays out of Portsmouth, and desperate to be at sea for longer, my father often found himself at home with time on his hands. At the end of January, he took Patricia and me into Southampton to have our photographs taken. We were each to have a turn wearing his naval "monkey jacket," the plan being to chart our growth through a series of photographs. In my first, the jacket came down to the floor, but Patricia, being fifteen, was showing rather a lot of leg. At the first attempt, the photographer obviously did not understand the purpose of the project because the prints arrived showing only our faces and upper bodies. Enraged at this incompetence, my father took us straight back to have our feet included. With an image of me smiling gleefully from my father's monkey jacket, this photo was to become one of my favorites, though it did come back to haunt me when my father came to Buckswood to show some lantern slides on the Royal Navy. I never forgave him for proclaiming, "And this, girls, is the final slide—a picture of a monkey in a monkey jacket."

By April 1940 there was mayhem in the seas around Norway and the Battle of France was brewing. HMS *Kelly* was ordered to sea. I went with my sister to have lunch on board the ship before our father departed. He showed us his cabin—which as always was decorated in exactly the same way as his bedrooms were on land; his desk was full of instruments and his bookshelves crammed with a complete war library of manuals and memoirs of service chiefs. I was worried that he had no novels—I would have been lost without mine—and planned to send him some while he was away. The day was tinged with a sense of foreboding, and although he made it enjoyable for us, the officers even giving us presents, I felt unsettled. When I got home, the only way I was able to express my fears was to scribble a note along the margin of my diary, in tiny writing as if I didn't want it to be real: "Daddy has gone to sea. Good luck to him."

Within a couple of weeks, Chamberlain resigned and Churchill took his place. Hitler's troops stormed through the Low Countries into France, horrifying the adults around me. I now wrote in my diary that "Daddy is having some awful adventures in the North Sea." When he came home in May 1940 I realized that this was no escapade—the *Kelly* had been torpedoed. What I didn't know at the time was that twenty-seven men had been killed and many more injured and that the blast had ripped a hole in her side that a double-decker bus could have been driven through. When she finally reached the Tyne, crowds cheered her all the way up the river. I later learned that my father had evacuated the rest of the crew from the ship, then he had crept back with only six officers and twelve men. Miraculously in a perilously listing ship, through three hundred miles of hostile seas, they had met with no further grave injury, despite being attacked by an enemy torpedo boat and strafed by German fighter planes. When I was taken to the cinema to watch the newsreels, I was immensely proud to see my father's heroic actions on the screen. We were all hugely relieved to have him back safely.

I knew, though, that my parents were worried about Bunny, who was fighting in northern France, and Yola, who was back at home, especially when Zelle told me that "Paris has fallen." My mother had heard nothing from Bunny for a while and from Broadlands we could see the flares from the explosions around Calais, twenty-two miles away across the Channel. Each distant flash made us anxious for the safety of our beloved Bunny.

It was in June 1940 when I was told, quite out of the blue, to pack my things at school and sent to meet up with my parents in London, that I knew things were about to change. On leaving school, I had stopped off overnight at Broadlands and thought there was something odd in Hanky's expression as she waved me off, but wasn't quite prepared for the look on my parents' faces as I entered the drawing room in Charles Street. Even though they were doing their best to hide it, they were clearly upset and, more worrying for me, so was my sister. Even Zelle was on the verge of tears. I thought someone close to us must have been killed in the war. They sat me down and my mother held my hand as she explained that Patricia and I were being sent to America until the end of the war. We were going to stay with someone very kind, a Mrs. Cornelius Vanderbilt, in New York. My father asked me to sign passports and other documents and told me that while Zelle didn't have the right paperwork to come with us just yet, they were doing their best to sort things out so she could join us.

I was so taken aback that I forgot to ask why we were being sent away, but I did manage to ask whether Lottie could come with us. Later, my sister explained that we were going because our great-grandfather, Ernest Cassell, had been Jewish, which meant that we were one-eighth Jewish. I nodded wisely but didn't really understand why that meant we had to leave our country and my beloved Lottie. I imagined it had something to do with Hitler but I didn't know for sure.

After frantic preparations—though my sister found time for a perm and even I was allowed to have my sides done—we said a very sad good-bye to my father, who had been given only a short leave from his ship to see us off. When we stood by our pile of trunks and cases in the hall to say good-bye to our mother, we were very tearful. She told Patricia, "When you get there, you must shake hands, the Americans do so all the time . . . and wear a bit of lipstick." With that, she pressed a pink lip salve into my sister's hand. She held us tight. She didn't need to say "Look after Pammy"; it was axiomatic that Patricia would care for me.

We left late that afternoon on a crowded train. Our parents had booked us passage from Ireland to the United States aboard SS *Washington*, the last ship to take children across the Atlantic before the crossing became too dangerous. Our distant cousin David—not my favorite little boy after he had bitten me following an argument in which he claimed that I had taken food for his dog and fed it to Lottie—and his Swiss mademoiselle were traveling with us as far as New York, and while at first we weren't happy about this, it was Mademoiselle who saved us when our paperwork was questioned in the west of Ireland. The officials were convinced only when they got hold of the British consul in Dublin, who verified our identity.

The ship was so full that some of the passengers had to sleep in the drained swimming pool. We shared a cabin with two other girls and a boy. The whole experience felt a bit unreal, but it soon turned into a great adventure: the very fact of being on a ship, the deck tennis, Ping-Pong, shuffleboard, and crazy golf. Not to mention all the animals belowdecks that I could pet and talk to. After a week at sea, Mademoiselle woke us up at dawn so that we could go out on deck as we sailed up the Hudson River. The Statue of Liberty was much taller than I had imagined. I had only ever seen pictures in magazines or on newsreels, so seeing it in reality was thrilling. Clearing customs, I was given my first taste of what being an "alien" meant. Having been born in Barcelona, I was made to stand in a different queue from Patricia and the rest of the English evacuees. The customs official told me—in a voice that I recognized from a hundred Hollywood movies—that under no circumstances could I work in America.

Cousin David and his mademoiselle left to meet their host family, and an extremely well-dressed woman introduced herself as Mrs. Vanderbilt's secretary. Even my childish eyes could see how fashionably she dressed, far better than anyone back home. She guided us into a waiting car and we were whisked towards 640 Fifth Avenue. The façade of Mrs. Vanderbilt's residence was enormous and imposing and the inside was no less so. The hall was cavernous, all marble floors and surfaces, and the huge malachite vase that was even taller than my sister made me feel like Alice in Wonderland. (Years later I was to see it again in the entrance hall of the Metropolitan Museum of Art.) A small queenly form—Mrs. Cornelius Vanderbilt was quite unlike anyone we had met before—came into view. She wore a long silk dress with a bandeau swathed around frizzy gray curls. "Ah, Patricia and Pamela, welcome to New York, my dears." Our hands shot out. "Good afternoon, Mrs. Vanderbilt," we said. "Oh, please," she said, taking our hands (but not shaking them), "girls, you must call me Aunt Grace." I wasn't sure I would be able to manage that—she seemed so imperious. "And this is my niece Anne." A glamorous lady in stockings, heels, and lipstick stepped towards us with an outstretched hand. "Anne is nearly your age, I believe, Patricia," Mrs. Vanderbilt added. For a second our eyes rounded with surprise. The "girl" could easily have passed for thirty. Beyond Mrs. Vanderbilt, at quite some distance, I could see footmen in dark-red livery darting here and there. I thought, America is going to be very different.

# 6

All through that hot summer of 1940 we were shunted among the Long Island summer houses of New York's kind society hostesses. While we were getting used to our new surroundings, unfamiliar American expressions, and new routines, the society hostesses were apparently trying to come to terms with how badly dressed we were. Mrs. Deering Howe was so disturbed by our appearance that within a few days several new dresses arrived. Patricia was disapproving—not only was there a war on and we shouldn't be concerned with such trivialities, but she knew at once that our mother would in no way wish us to accept these gifts. I thought they were divinely pretty and desperately wanted to keep them. But it was not to be. We had to decline the offer and wait for some money to come through from our parents.

I wrote copious letters from Mrs. Vanderbilt's villa-style residence on Bellevue Avenue, Newport, Rhode Island. I wrote to my mother and to my father, who insisted that all letters be numbered in case some of them arrived out of sequence or were lost at sea, and also that I should write alternately to him and my mother. This made it difficult sometimes when I was in the mood to tell my news to one before the other, only to find it wasn't their turn. I also wrote to Grandmama and Hanky.

As the war progressed, I felt guilty being so safe when our parents were not. My mother's job involved driving around at night after bombs had dropped, helping people in the shelters as well as improving the facilities available to the emergency services. She wrote that we were not to worry about her as she had become quite "nippy" at avoiding danger. She actually seemed to be enjoying herself.

I couldn't unburden my feelings of homesickness to my mother because she was so easily upset and it was always, as in our home life, more straightforward to share our worries with our father. I drew a picture for him and posted it with letter number 14, showing "Pamela Carmen Louise" stranded on a raft—"floating to you!" There were three flags on this vessel: one simply had the word "Help," the second displayed the Union Jack, and the third, quite obviously, was a pair of billowing bloomers labeled "white pants." The jolliness was a poor attempt to hide the slight but ever-present feeling that I missed home.

In turn we received letters from our father and Hanky and Bunny. The King of the Moon was in fine form, lacing his letters with stories and sweet sentiments. As she dashed around, our mother sent us several cables with news of her war effort. I was especially pleased to hear from Hanky, who gave us longed-for news of the dogs. I was still feeling guilty that during one of our good-byes, I had pulled away from her, suddenly unwilling to be kissed by the prickly, almost invisible mustache on her top lip. She had always been so warm and giving, and sometimes before I went to sleep I imagined her back at Broadlands, upset and mystified by my rudeness. I made sure that I wrote to her with a lot of affection in my letters, telling her that I couldn't wait to see her again.

The best news came in the form of a cable announcing Zelle's imminent arrival. Until now, we had been under the care of a Mrs. Gertrude Pugh, a thoroughly English, unsympathetic woman who wore long pink boudoir knickers that came down to her knees (hiding from her one afternoon, Patricia and I spotted these under her skirt from our refuge under the bed). It was such a relief when Zelle replaced Miss Pugh, bringing with her news, letters, and presents from the family. Being with Zelle did also have its downside—I was allowed to speak to her and Patricia only in French during the day. If I hadn't spoken any English by nightfall, I was given a cent.

When the summer came to an end, we returned to Manhattan with Mrs. Vanderbilt. While, of course, we lived a privileged life at Broadlands, I wasn't quite prepared for the relentless grandeur and ostentation of Mrs. Vanderbilt's lifestyle, this manifestation of the excesses of New York "society." There was nothing she liked more than to talk of the British aristocracy, and I think our link to the royal family really thrilled her. One morning, when we had just started school, she pulled us both out of lessons to see the sumptuous lunch table she had arranged for the British ambassador, Lord Halifax. An enthusiastic Mrs. Vanderbilt escorted us into the large paneled dining room, allowing me to take a sugar-dusted marshmallow from one of the ornate silver bowls, utterly convinced that seeing her table setting was an essential part of a young girl's education. My parents were horrified at a newspaper headline about "royal refugees" going to the races with Mrs. Cornelius Vanderbilt, and the gossip columns ran a story about how, morning and evening, you could spot the "well-born evacuees" walking down Fifth Avenue. In fact the walk to our schools each morning was the highlight of my day for, if it wasn't raining, Zelle would buy us a brioche and a slab of chocolate that we would eat on a bench in Central Park, while the pastry was still warm.

School in America was an eye-opener. After fielding such questions as "Do you have electricity in England?"; forcing myself to tolerate the endless mimicking of my accent; convincing the girls that Patricia and I did not shorten our names to "Pat" and "Pam"; and history being turned upside down—from the American Revolution to the War of Independence and finding that all the goodies had become baddies—I was astonished that during "recess" my fellow classmates undertook a ferocious shoplifting competition at the local "drugstore." I would rather have died than steal something, so I removed myself to the soda fountain. As at school back home, I found it stressful being with so many girls each and every day, until during an afternoon game of tag—the sole aim of which seemed to be to push over as many people as possible—I noticed another girl, Anne de Rothschild, who seemed to prefer to play on her own. We became firm friends and played happily and quietly together. After a couple of weeks I was taken aside and told it really might be better for me not to play with her. I racked my brains as to why until I realized: however wealthy you were at this school, if you were Jewish you would always be seen as different. They obviously did not know that I had Jewish ancestors, and I continued to play with Anne.

Despite attending school, being with Patricia and Zelle, and receiving the kindness of the impeccably behaved New Yorkers, I couldn't settle, especially as news of my father's "adventures"—family code for life-threatening events—reached us. Southampton had been heavily bombed, as had Brook House again (luckily no one was there at the time and all the main furniture, pictures, and even the Whistler panels in the boudoir had been put into storage at the beginning of the war). I felt bad, here in what seemed like another world, as if I should be back at home suffering like everybody else. I wasn't exactly unhappy to begin with—there were too many new experiences and things that made Patricia and me laugh. For example, it was important for Mrs. Vanderbilt to be seen at the opera and she decided to take Patricia with her—that is, to some of the opera. Eager to make an entrance, Mrs. Vanderbilt would never arrive until the end of the first act, whereupon she would enter her box with the diamonds of her sumptuous Cartier necklace ablaze as the lights went up for the interval. After she felt that she had been noticed sufficiently, she would take her seat. At the end of the second act, Mrs. Vanderbilt felt she had done her bit and would go home, so Patricia got to know only the second act of the operas. But what made me chuckle even more than this was the story that Mrs. Vanderbilt had once given a dinner party when the Royal Shakespeare Company were playing in New York. A young man at her table had apologized and asked whether he might be excused from the table because he was going to see *Hamlet*. Mrs. Vanderbilt had looked slightly nonplussed and so he explained, "Hamlet, Prince of Denmark," whereupon her face lit up and she exclaimed loudly, so that everyone could hear, "Oh, do give the dear boy my good wishes. I knew his father so well."

Letters from home were becoming less frequent and they often arrived in a mixed-up order. Our mother wrote to tell us that the baby wallaby had died and then we received another from her that said he was doing very well. A week or so later a third letter arrived to tell us that it had been born. It was a very difficult time for everyone, and perhaps the fact that there seemed to be no end in sight to the conflict prompted both Bunny and then my father to write tender words of advice to me. Bunny's letter was particularly touching. He wrote: "Darling Plonk, I have just got a new job in London—I am now more or less in charge of this WAR so it should be over very soon. I saw your Papa last night for the first time in some months. He is looking very well, your poor Mama on the other hand has had a bad cold in di noze. I have sadly not seen any of yours or Plinks's masterpiece letters lately but I hope to next weekend when I go to Broadlands. Getting your letters has made all the difference to the happiness of your doting parents during these long months since your departure. Wasn't it a tragedy that this babe died [here, Bunny had drawn a picture of a wallaby]. You have never seen anything so sweet as it was. I do hope Babo produces another soon. Everyone misses you both so very much and longs for your return. Remember to get all the fun that you can out of your trip, as you may never get such a carefree time again. I will try to write a little more often . . . Bless you and tons of love from H M Rex Luna."

On 27 May 1941, Zelle came to take Patricia and me home from school as usual. What I didn't know was that Zelle had already broken the news to my sister that our father's ship, HMS *Kelly*, had been bombed in Crete and half the crew were missing, presumed dead. Patricia had managed to let out her first wave of tears before I came out of school and she composed herself before meeting me. I was terribly shocked when Zelle told me, while we were traveling home on the bus, that my father was missing. I let out such a loud wail that the bus came to a stop. By the evening I was numb with terror. In the middle of the night, Zelle came and woke us with the news that he had survived. My mother had sent a cable as soon as she heard. I got up at once and wrote her a thank-you letter. I was so relieved that I forgot to put a number on the letter but thought my father wouldn't mind just this once.

By some miracle, my parents were able to visit us that summer. When I heard this news, it seemed too good to be true and the heartache of the last twelve months lifted. I looked out of the window from my summer bedroom on Long Island, at the great yachts and little sailing boats bobbing on Oyster Bay, and as the lights twinkled from the buildings opposite the shore, I realized that for the first time in a very long while, I was happy.

My parents arrived in mid-August and we drove out to upstate New York and took up temporary residence in a flat lent to us by friends. We all noticed how Patricia was now taller than our mother but were careful not to draw attention to it. Mummy, however, seemed not in a mood to be offended. We spent six glorious days together, catching up on our news, visiting places, and talking about how we would all be together as soon as the war was over. Then my parents had to get on with their work. My mother was about to depart on a speaking tour of the United States, ostensibly as a goodwill gesture to thank the American Red Cross for all their help, but her intention was also to inform the Americans about what was really going on in Britain. Lady Louis Mountbatten was a big-enough name to pull in a crowd, and she had a lot of firsthand experience of the horrors of the Blitz. The night before she left she produced a speech that she had carefully written out by hand and was planning to read. My father shocked us all by tearing it up. "No, Snooky.

You'll bore them all rigid." Instead he persuaded her to learn it and showed her how to make prompting notes. "You'll be terrific," he said, kissing her. She did as he said and later we learned that the tour was an unqualified success. She always attributed her ability to speak in public to the confidence my father placed in her, and was acknowledged as a fine speaker.

My father, meanwhile, was to travel down to Norfolk, Virginia, to inspect the aircraft carrier HMS *Illustrious* before he took command of her. Before that he paid a flying visit to Pearl Harbor and was not impressed by the poor state of readiness and general lack of cooperation between the US Navy and the US Army. He lamented the absence of a joint HQ, and on his return he described something that had shocked him—all the American aircraft had been lined up in rows, leaving them vulnerable to attack. When he pointed this out to those in command, his advice fell on deaf ears. He was so agitated that at the breakfast table he couldn't stop until he talked himself out. Once he had done so, he dispatched his fried egg in two gulps and gave me a sort of consolation pat on the shoulders as he left the table. My father's plans changed when he was suddenly called back to England. He gave us no indication of what he was up to and we were terribly sad to see him go. Later, in one of his many letters to us, he explained that Churchill had ordered him to return to take over as chief of Combined Operations. This was a complex job—coordinating all the top naval, military, and air experts and chiefs of the Royal Navy, the Army, and the Royal Air Force in planning, equipping, and training for offensive operations.

My mother was able to take a break from her tour and took Patricia and me for a bus trip to the country—although at first we took the state hospital bus by mistake. A couple of weeks before she was to return to England, Bunny arrived. He had been sent to New York as an intelligence officer. It was lovely to have him come to visit us and we all went to the movies to see *How Green Was My Valley* and then, when that made us all sad, to the new Walt Disney film *Dumbo*, which of course I loved.

It was not long before Bunny saw what my parents had failed to see: that I was miserable in America, being cooped up with Zelle and her unrelenting French. He and my mother had several conversations with my sister in which Bunny argued that it would be far better for me to face the bombs in England and be happy than to stay here and feel wretched. Patricia decided that as there were only six months until she graduated from high school, it was important she should stay so she could leave with qualifications. She agreed that it would be best for me to return to England with my mother.

On 26 November we arrived at LaGuardia at seven in the morning. The press had also got up early that morning and their presence rather curtailed an emotional good-bye with Patricia. We ended up smiling inanely at each other, giving the photographers some posed shots: she, a sophisticated young woman, tall and elegant, carrying a neat little handbag and white gloves, and me, a child in a little short-sleeved dress with a white collar, wearing a black beret and with a white cardigan draped over my left arm, just as Mrs. Vanderbilt had taught me. You might have thought we were relaxed and calm, but if you looked closely you could see that I was gripping my sister's hand, gripping it hard, as if I never wanted to let go.

My mother and I flew to Bermuda. I wrote letter number 1 to Patricia. Then on to Lisbon, where I wrote letter number 2 to Patricia. Unfortunately my place on the London leg of the journey was suddenly required for the mail, and when the plane stopped for refueling, I was told I would have to remain in Lisbon for another ten days. My mother arranged for the naval attaché and his wife to look after me and I ended up having a good time with Commander and Mrs. Billyard-Leake and their *twelve* dogs. Someone told me that I was one of two thousand people waiting for a flight, and I saw in a flash that a twelve-and-a-half-year-old just might not be a priority to the war effort.

The day before I left, the Japanese attacked the American fleet at Pearl Harbor. As I boarded the plane to complete my journey home, both the country that had hosted me for over a year and the country to which I was returning declared war on Japan. I was worried about Patricia and longed for her to come home too.

7

Broadlands had been transformed. It was now an annex to the Royal Southampton Hospital, humming with civilian ambulances and nurses buzzing about in starched white uniforms. There were men and women walking around in slippers and dressing gowns, together with a rather alarming white shed, protruding from the central columns of the Georgian portico, in which bedpans were washed out and cleaned. It all seemed very strange, and although I was curious, I knew I must not get in the way and kept to our private wing.

Having been president of the Hampshire Division, my mother was now superintended in chief of the St. John Ambulance Brigade Nursing Division, the highest position a woman could hold. She was responsible for the supervision of mobile medical units, rest centers, first aid, and medical posts in the underground shelters; forever away in towns and cities across the country organizing sixty thousand volunteers and ten thousand cadets and visiting convalescent homes, blood-transfusion centers, hospitals, and air-raid precaution posts. In London, if she wasn't driving out to the scene of a horrific bombing, she was on the roof of the Joint War Organisation's headquarters, watching for incendiaries.

Back in Broadlands it was impossible not to be aware of the loud drone of the German bombers returning from their missions over London as they jettisoned their unused bombs over our park and estate—luckily some considerable distance from the house—before flying back across the English Channel. As one of England's most important ports, Southampton suffered catastrophic destruction from bombs and I would say a prayer, asking God to spare people's lives, as I saw the afterglow of the raids from my bedroom window. Finally, following several weeks of bombardment, the city authorities constructed an enormous "lure" at the edge of the Broadlands estate that was lit at night with the intention of confusing enemy bombers into thinking it was Southampton. Mr. Diment, who farmed at the edge of the estate, came to tell us he was delighted that "defenses" were being built to protect him. His face dropped when my father explained it was precisely the opposite, that the bombs might soon be falling a little closer to him.

Out riding one afternoon, I watched two planes locked in a fight high above the Hampshire Downs, and a few weeks later, a German Heinkel crashed on nearby Green Hill, killing all the crew. The previous year, while I was still in New York, a Messerschmitt had been shot down over Town Copse, the pieces falling near Home Farm. As soon as Grandmama heard the news, she rushed out with the sole intention of taking the propeller. She was terribly annoyed to find that someone else had got there before her. Just as well—the propeller would have been much larger than her small frame, certainly too heavy for her to drag all the way home. She did salvage several chunks of metal, however, two bits of which my father had mounted on silver boxes that were inscribed for Patricia and me. I kept mine proudly on my dressing table, a tiny trophy.

It was wonderful to see Hanky again, although many of the other familiar faces had either vanished or been conscripted. I felt much happier back in Broadlands, away from the loneliness of the past year. Compared to living in New York, everything here felt so real, especially down at Home Farm. I loved to take the dogs down there, particularly if the blacksmith was shoeing at the forge. I watched the cows being milked, let the calves suck on my fingers, and stood mesmerized by the sawmill, cheerfully dodging the wood-cuttings. My grandfather's black-and-white Friesian cows, which at night looked liked a group of sheets floating about in the field, had not been tested for tuberculosis, so had to be replaced by a herd of Guernseys that were much better milk producers. My mother had heard that Suffolk punches were dying out, so she had recently bought some for breeding. Sadly the experiment was a disaster because, unlike our docile shire horses, these feisty beasts kept running away with the plow.

For the first time in his naval career my father was neither at sea nor bound for it. As chief of Combined Operations, he was now a commodore, and the four gold rings of captain had been replaced by a dazzling broad gold stripe on both his sleeves. He was busy planning the Commando raids against enemy territory, all very hush-hush. We heard from Patricia regularly—she was doing well in her classes, working hard towards her exams. Bunny also continued to be a good correspondent, writing of his new posting to Washington. One of his first tasks had been to break into the safe at the German embassy—it had been completely empty except for the keys to the British embassy's safe. We had heard little from Yola in occupied France but we did know she was still alive. A few letters had trickled through but they were simply dated *"jeudi matin"* or *"vendredi soir"* with no hint of a date, month, or year, which naturally drove my father to distraction.

As always, there was a constant flow of guests, which sorely tested the humor of Hanky, Chef, and our butler Frank, as they had little help. Now that my mother had become "serious," all our visitors were too. Our guests were now usually serving officers or people whose help my parents wanted to enlist in some way. My father's flag lieutenant was often at Broadlands and once my father invited the most senior officer in the Royal Navy, the first sea lord, to come for a quiet weekend, "to get away from it all." It didn't quite go to plan—during the night so many incendiary bombs fell that the poor man's bedroom window was constantly lit up by flashes and he had little sleep. Peter Murphy was still a regular, and luckily some of the serious guests were good fun too. My godfather, Prince George, the Duke of Kent, was just such a visitor. He and my mother got on very well, sharing an interest in the arts. He came down to stay just after Christmas and I accompanied them both on a visit to the hospital wards next door. There I saw at first hand how brilliant my mother was as she talked to the patients—she always had something to say, a genuine expression of concern or a cheering remark, and she had an innate sense of just how long she should stay and when to move on. Everyone we met seemed not only delighted to welcome her but also massively cheered to be visited by a member of the royal family. I followed silently behind, in my smart wool dress and thick brown lisle stockings, proud to see what a difference my mother could make.

As 1942 drew to a close, my parents told me that from the New Year, I was to attend Miss Faunce's PNEU—Parents' National Education Union—School in Dorset. My cousin Mary Anna, whom I had never met before, was a pupil there.

Mary Anna was now an orphan, her mother having died when she was very young and her father dying in Cairo less than a year before we met. Now she was cared for by her guardian and his family. They lived in Crichel, her enormous Palladian family home, and she was both understanding and outraged that her relatives were using all her family's china, silver, and bed linen. "And," she added with great irritation, "it's *ridiculous* that they've allowed Bryanstone, a *boys'* school, in . . . But don't worry, Pammy, I'll get them out." Mary Anna was strong-willed and not afraid to voice her opinions—she was like a breath of fresh air and we quickly became best friends.

Miss Faunce's school had been evacuated from London and was now situated in St. Giles House, the Dorset home of Lord and Lady Shaftesbury, who also happened to be Mary Anna's grandparents. She spent as much time as she could with them in their private wing, much to the resentment of her guardian and his wife. It was easy to see why she was so happy in their company, as Cousin Tono and Cousin Cuckoo (as I knew them) were eccentric and affectionate, and they adored their granddaughter. We sixty or so Fauncites saw them regularly—especially in church on Sunday. Cousin Cuckoo often popped into our classrooms to say hello or to leave food out for the mice. She carried off a distinctive look—she wore white woolen stockings and bronze pumps with bows on, her hair was always braided and coiled around her ears like earmuffs, and she was accompanied either by a beautifully behaved black chow or a wretched little Yorkshire terrier that would bite you at every opportunity. She was a bit of a maverick—distributing food to anyone in the village who might need it, while also smuggling in supplies of Jersey cream, a somewhat embarrassing incident for her husband, who was lord lieutenant of Dorset.

I enjoyed school—it was structured and the teaching, across the disciplines, was stimulating. The overriding philosophy was that we should be inspired by as broad a curriculum as possible. So, in addition to my favorite subjects of English, history, and Scripture, I was privileged to be taught botany, the myths of Greece, Rome, and Scandinavia, picture study, ballet, ballroom and tap dancing, as well as receiving the once-a-week update on the progress of the war, using maps and newspapers. As the school was now in the magnificent grounds of St. Giles, with its avenues of beech trees, a lake, and outlying fields and woods, we had to go for an early-morning run six days a week—quite a shock to my system. Miss Faunce was a small powerhouse of a woman who was such a brilliant speaker that, when she read to us, the characters danced off the page. We were filled with dread by her instruction in narration, however, during which we had to take terrifying turns, standing up and paraphrasing back to the class what we had just been taught. Unfortunately Miss Faunce—who always wore black and smelled of death—did not like me much, describing my behavior as "wild and uncontrolled" in my end-of-term report. Unlike Patricia, who had been head girl, I did not register as one of her favorites; indeed, I even overheard her telling another teacher, "That Pamela Mountbatten, you would never know she was Patricia's sister." Every night we had to say good night to her by shaking her hand and curtsying, and if she was displeased with you for some reason, she would curtail the handshake by shoving your hand away without looking in your eyes. She rarely looked me in the eye.

The Shaftesburys were very High Church and insisted that the school respect this. Even though we were all Anglicans, we had to address the priest as "Father" Janson-Smith. As the church was within the school grounds we saw him regularly but we weren't allowed to talk to him if he was on his way to give someone communion. Cousin Cuckoo went to church three times on a Sunday, her smaller dog, Simmy, the Yorkshire terrier, always tucked under her arm, and for the early-morning service she would set off in a sheepskin coat and a yellow bath hat that was intended to hide her curlers. By the eleven o'clock service she was in her best clothes, hair neatly coiled, and this would last until evensong, where she would inevitably be engaged in a battle with Mary Anna, who would stand rigidly upright as her grandmother tugged at her skirt trying to get her to genuflect. Thanks to Cousin Tono's insistence, the incense, swung around with gusto by the altar boys, was so strong that often one of the girls became dizzy and fainted.

The first winter of my school attendance included the coldest February since 1914; the water on our bedside tables froze as we slept and there was a mass outbreak of chilblains. Combined with the rationing of food, heating, and bathwater—we were allowed a bath only three times a week and the water level could not come above the five-inch mark that was clearly painted inside the tub—it was a pretty miserable few months. As Miss Faunce said, however, "If it's good enough for the king . . ." and we were certainly not alone, suffering with everyone else in the country. Even my mother, usually insulated by her wealth, ran out of fuel and had to live without heating or hot water. We also knew—being well-informed Fauncites—that our discomfort was nothing compared to that being suffered by our troops. Once again, I was enthusiastically "knitting for the navy," and this time the recipient of my scarf, one Engineer Slater, took the trouble to write and thank me. I was thrilled to bits.

The horror of war did not intrude too much. We learned what to do in the event of a bombing raid—throw ourselves to the ground, lie flat on the floor, and leave our mouths slightly agape until the teachers had checked with their fingers to see whether they were open wide enough. Our gas masks were tested from time to time down on the village green by a man with a strange sort of van, and if the sirens sounded near by, the teachers would summon us by calling out "Chocolate and biscuits in the cellars, darlings!" If it was nighttime we would grab the dressing gown belt of the girl in front and walk quietly downstairs. In the daytime the cook would serve up lunch or supper and as soon as the food appeared, our favorite occupation was to pull the stringy fat off our meat and poke it into the cavities of the cellar walls behind us. All this was tedious rather than exciting, and even rumors that a mother had supplied Miss Faunce with a gun in case of an invasion did little to stir us. We were young girls, on the cusp of adolescence, more excited by the rare appearance of a man than by wartime logistics.

Actually, men were so rare that when the dance teacher brought her uniformed fiancé to the school, excitement bubbled contagiously along the corridors. When John Ashley Cooper, the Shaftesburys' youngest son, returned home on leave, excitement levels reached such heights that we all hung out of the windows trying to catch a glimpse of him—even Mary Anna, and he was her uncle. After he had been back for a week or so, a few of us were summoned to Miss Faunce's office. She accused one of us—and she was going to wait until the culprit owned up—of sneaking down to the lake to watch John Ashley Cooper fishing. As none of us had actually committed this terrible sin (I stood there thinking, Why didn't I think of that?), we stood in painful silence as Miss

Faunce turned to Anne Maude: "Your father is a lawyer. You must say what you think has happened." I was glad my father was in the navy.

As we traveled home for Easter, I was met off the train by my father's good-looking flag lieutenant, which left my traveling companions somewhat speechless. And things only got better. My father had arranged for me to attend filming of Noël Coward's *In Which We Serve*, which was based upon my father's adventures in HMS *Kelly*, on the day when the king and queen and the two princesses were also due to visit the studio. I went in the car with the girls, and as we drove through the small crowd that had gathered near the studio, Princess Elizabeth kept reminding her sister that she "really must *wave* at the people." Noël was in his element that day—he adored being center stage, even if he did have to share it with the king—and we were allowed to stand on the "deck" as the storm scene was being prepared. The deck had been constructed so that it could pitch and roll in the "swell," and after a few minutes the princesses and I felt so sick we asked whether we could climb down. Although at first the Admiralty and the Ministry of Defence had been dead against a film showing a British ship being sunk, the film went ahead, and in fact turned out to be a huge and lasting success.

My parents had some entertaining friends, none more so than Douglas Fairbanks Jr., who had been assigned from the US Navy to my father's Commando staff. He was as dazzling as a film star should be and a joy to be around, full of laughter and good stories. I loved the one about the sergeant and the wall, especially the lively way that he told it: "You see, Pammy, when I was training over here we had to do this hellish exercise. You know, running around over and over, under and under, over and under, that kind of thing. And at the end there was this enormous wall. Impassable, as far as I was concerned. So I just stood there, catching my breath, working out how to get over the damn thing, and my sergeant comes up and yells, 'Come on, Fairbanks, over you go. Like in the films, you've done it before.'"

Patricia returned from America that June and came down to see me at school. She was eighteen and seemed very grown up to me. It was such a comfort to have her back—I was jittery from having witnessed a low-flying aircraft drag a man tangled up in his parachute, who was later found dead in Poole Harbour—and I felt reassured by her presence. She immediately caught on that I was the only girl not wearing a Sunday dress, and when I admitted that I was indeed the only girl who didn't own a Sunday dress, she had one sent to me by the time the next Sunday came around. I was pretty self-sufficient, having had to rely on myself for so long, but it was always a relief to know Patricia was there for me.

I wasn't exactly sure what my parents' work really involved. I could imagine my mother improving conditions for Londoners at the mercy of the bombings but had never seen her at work outside of Southampton. The precise details of my father's responsibilities were necessarily secret, and although his name came up on the news broadcasts that I watched with my classmates, I was not aware that he was overseeing plans for the invasion of Europe. When I learned that there had been a "big Commando raid on Dieppe" I could only guess at my father's involvement.

On her return, Patricia had joined the Women's Royal Naval Service, qualifying soon after as a signals rating. She was positioned at the Combined Operations base HMS *Tormentor* at Warsash, just east of Southampton, and during my next visit home, I jumped on the bus with my bike, then cycled down—as quickly as I could, she had saved me a Mars bar!—to see her. I was almost as excited by the prospect of the chocolate bar as I was by that of seeing my beloved sister, but when the moment came, we discovered a mouse had nibbled half of it away. Later I was pleased to report back to Hanky, who was missing Patricia deeply, that the remaining half was definitely worth the journey.

At thirteen and home for the summer holidays, I needed to play my part in the war effort too. My grandmother had given me a lovely black-and-white pony and together we managed to get hold of an old dogcart which, with a new coat of paint and some varnish, was soon restored to its former glory. Chiquita and I were thereafter purposefully employed, running errands and proudly circumventing the fuel shortage. We picked people up from the station and took flowers to the St. John's shop in Romsey to help raise funds. Our route often took us by the local prisoner-of-war camp, known as "Ganger Camp," which housed Italian and German POWs. The camp's Nissen huts were well defended behind tall wire fences with gun batteries and a machine-gun post, and when the prisoners were out working on the local farms, they were watched over by a soldier with a gun. On one occasion, I noticed a Tommy reach into his pocket for a light. Fumbling a little, he passed his gun to a prisoner to hold for him while he lit his cigarette. He took a long, relaxed puff, then stuck out his arm, and his gun was gently handed back.

After I had been making the daily journey into Romsey for a couple of weeks, a young Italian hailed me from a field. To my utter surprise he presented me with a ring made out of shiny metal. I felt my cheeks heat up as I stammered a thank-you in my best Italian. It was the first ring I had ever been given, and when I examined it in the privacy of my room, I was amazed to see how intricate it was, how the man had somehow carved a little pattern on it. I never saw him again but I wore the ring proudly.

Every prisoner could work if he so wished. Most helped on local farms, hedging, ditching, and doing seasonal chores, and they became very much part of the landscape, as our farmworkers were away at war. That August, 1943, it was all hands to the pump as Grandmama and I worked with them to bring in the harvest. Even my mother came down to lend a hand for three days. As the workhorses drew the harvester across the hundred-acre field, trailing long uneven lines of hay in its wake, we walked behind gathering the hay into stooks and securing them with string. Grandmama was an old lady, yet she insisted on being involved, though she couldn't tie the string as her fingers were stiff and swollen with chilblains. I tied hers for her. The Italian men watched us and I wondered whether the presence of my grandmother made them think of their own families; whether my glamorous-looking mother in her corduroy slacks and scarf fixed decorously over her hair made them think of the women they had left behind. I hoped they didn't notice me—my prickled legs and bleeding fore-arms made me feel distinctly less than glamorous.

Putting my pony trap to good use and helping bring in the harvest gave me huge satisfaction, and I felt useful and productive from spending so much time outdoors. The war showed no sign of abating and tragedy struck when my god-father, the Duke of Kent, was killed in an air accident. He had been on his way—in thick fog—to Iceland on an RAF mission, when the Sunderland flying boat in which he was being flown crashed into a Scottish hillside in Caithness. I was very shocked by this news—he and his ADC, Michael Strutt, had stayed with us only two weeks earlier and now both men had been killed. This was what was meant by the fragility of life, I thought, and I prayed that such a fate would not befall my father.

When the British and American forces invaded French North Africa, I recorded optimistically in my diary, "The war news is wonderful—about Libya and Egypt. Our Forces have driven the Germans back over the Egyptian border. We hope that the war over there is almost over." This hope was echoed by Winston Churchill in his dramatic speech the following day, words I turned over and over in my mind: "This is not the end. It is not even the beginning of the end. But it is, perhaps, the end of the beginning." Allied success in Egypt did mean that a week later church bells rang all over the country for twenty minutes. Hearing them at St. Giles made me realize that I had never heard the sound of bells at Broadlands, as they'd been silenced at the beginning of the war under strict instruction that they should be rung only in the event of an invasion. That Sunday I felt optimistic, at least that the tide was turning. But waking the next morning to learn that "hit-and-run" raids had been carried out in twenty towns across southern England brought the harsh reality crashing back.

We had to get on as best we could. When, at Christmas, my mother was so preoccupied guarding a precious ham that General Marshall had given her she left all our presents on the train, I didn't complain. Actually, even if I had, no one would have listened: the loss of the presents paled into insignificance when my mother realized her nearly completed five-year diary was also still on the train. Both my parents were left worrying that we would come to see its contents in print and this sparked some lively conversations around the dinner table. My mother, always enterprising, paid a flying visit to London in a frantic search for replacement presents.

As a result of her tireless work my mother was made a CBE in the New Year Honours; Patricia was now a fully fledged Wren and my father was at the heart of Britain's war strategy. In fact, owing to overwork, he had recently succumbed to jaundice and pneumonia, worrying us all. He was well enough to discuss strategy with General Eisenhower but was unusually anxious that the visit should go smoothly. So it was with alarm that we watched as the great man's huge Cadillac veered off the drive and stopped dead in the ditch, trying to negotiate the awkward angle of the garden gates, which had now become our front entrance.

As well as being a hospital annex, Broadlands became a training encampment for the US troops of the Fourth Division. Even though this was the division's "laundry unit," many of these soldiers became frontline troops soon enough, going to their untimely deaths in France. Then yet more Americans were billeted at the end of the drive, when Lee Park House was given over to the Pioneer Corps. My parents invited them up to the house. Despite my time in America, I was astounded by the relaxed attitude of the soldiers to their superiors—being used to the rigid naval forms of "Yes, sir," "No, sir," I found their way of addressing their commanding officer as "Colonel Jack" or just "Jack" shocking. They were fun to have around, though, and were fascinated to see inside Broadlands, asking endless questions. When I was asked who had painted the eighteenth-century panels depicting classical scenes on the ceiling of the drawing room, I answered "Helena Rubinstein." The effect was electric. "Say, is that so?!" exclaimed my impressed audience. "We had no idea she did that sort of thing. Joe, come take a look—gee, who'd have guessed it was Helena Rubinstein!" The moment I had said it, I realized my mistake, but I was too embarrassed to tell them it was of course the ubiquitous Angelica Kauffmann. One time, over in Britain to entertain the American troops, Irving Berlin accompanied the soldiers to the house. Grandmama was delighted to meet him, as Grandpapa had been to a restaurant in New York when Irving Berlin was a singing waiter.

Life in the midst of all this activity could be vexing. Security at the American encampment soon became so tight that Grandmama and Isa could not come to stay with us until we had obtained a special permit allowing them to pass through. At the time my father was away—he had been appointed Supreme Allied Commander, South-East Asia, to try to reverse the disastrous gains the Japanese had made in Burma—and Bunny was also bound for the South-East Asia Command (SEAC), so my mother had to deal with all the red tape herself. This was also when poor Isa suffered another disaster. Having been sent a packet of dehydrated bananas from America, she mistook them for crystallized fruit and, nibbling one, she found it so delicious she finished most of the packet. She then needed a long drink of water. The bananas swelled up inside her and her stomach nearly exploded.

For several months during the war, the whole area of Southampton was closed to anyone not living or working there. Broadlands was just within the fifteen-mile exclusion zone. The buildup of troops, vehicles, and temporary camps in the area was enormous, and as the weather improved in the late spring there was an air of expectation. Suddenly, as quickly as they had arrived, the American soldiers left Broadlands. D-Day had finally come.

## 8

As a signals rating at HMS *Tormentor*, Patricia was privy to all sorts of information regarding preparations for D-Day, as all the orders and plans had passed through her office. But she knew that "Loose Tongues Cost Lives," and so the rest of us didn't know anything until Operation Overlord had taken place. On one of her monthly one-night sleep-out passes, I sat listening, electrified, as she told us about the planning and the subsequent success and horror stories.

It transpired that in the final days before the Normandy invasion, there had been such a buildup of ships—astonishingly, around seven hundred—on the Hamble that Patricia said she could have walked from the bay beyond Southampton to the Isle of Wight without getting a foot wet. Over the past year, she and her fellow Wrens had become friendly with the soldiers based on the smaller flotillas, who had been running reconnaissance missions, so when they heard news of the impending action, they felt terribly anxious as to the fate of these young men. On 5 June they had embarked Lord Lovat from the Hamble with his famous piper and his Commandos in their landing craft. Thousands of other vessels of every kind and over seven hundred warships were waiting for the signal to depart, but bad weather prevented action. On the clear morning of 6 June, however, when General Eisenhower gave the order, my sister watched as the boats disappeared in the direction of Normandy, dragging hundreds of barrage balloons with them, and with squadrons of fighter planes droning overhead. As the day progressed, the sound of bombing and gunfire from across the Channel was clearly audible and, tearfully, Patricia described her fears as she and her colleagues waited for the survivors to return. Sadly, many of the young men died in the Battle of Normandy, and as she spoke, I realized with a start that many of the young men of the "laundry unit" would have lost their lives too.

We all hoped that D-Day would mean the end of the war but still it dragged on, with a new type of danger now in the V-I "doodlebugs" that began to fall over England, killing hundreds of people. When I was in our London base in Chester Street, I could hear them drone slowly through the sky, high above the house. But as I lay in bed in the darkness, I reminded myself: you are safe if you can hear them. It was when the engine cut out that you knew the bomb was about to drop. That was when it was really frightening. Anyway, I was finding it difficult to sleep wherever I was since I'd received the shocking news that Hanky had died after an operation. I was told at school, and when I burst into floods of tears, the mistress said irritably, "But *who* is Hanky?" I felt so angry with her for asking this, because to me Hanky was nearly *everything*. My friends were solicitous and gathered round me protectively, but for a while I felt torn apart with grief.

As if this weren't enough, when Bunny was next on leave, he dropped a huge bombshell—revealing that he was engaged to my aunt Nada and late uncle George's niece, Gina. My mother took the news very badly and there were times in the ensuing weeks, as she took endless dismal walks alone down

Adsdean. Patricia and I wearing jaunty French hats given to us by Yola Letellier

Family at Brook House, 1940

My grandmother Princess Victoria of Hesse and by Rhine, later Marchioness of Milford Haven

My donkey in Malta, 1932

As a Brownie with Lottie in Malta, 1935

Our shelter at Kekes, 1935

Princess Plink and Princess Plonk with the Queen of the Moon

Bunny returning home with Sabi the lion

At Newport's Casino. Mrs. Cornelius Vanderbilt, and her guests "for the duration," the Honorable Pamela Mountbatten and the Honorable Patricia Mountbatten, kin of George VI. At right her grandchild, Cornelia Davis. Photos: Bert Morgan.

Snowballing in Central Park, 1941

My parents in uniform, 1939

Broadlands with the dogs, Mizzen and Jib, 1942

the river path, when my father and my sister feared she might drown herself. It was no good bringing up Bunny's departure with her directly—she was never open to any conversation about relationship or feelings and had trained herself as a child to be self-sufficient. Patricia wrote a short but heart-felt letter to our brittle and sensitive mother, however, and this seemed to do something to short-circuit the unbearable loneliness she was feeling. Just composing this letter, thinking about how she was suffering, made Patricia feel closer to my mother than she had ever felt before. Of course, Bunny made constant—and ultimately successful—efforts to prevent the deep friendship that existed between us from being broken. He even asked me to be a bridesmaid at his wedding. I was overjoyed, as I had never been a bridesmaid before, but my mother told me firmly, without looking in her diary, that I would be at school that day and it would not be possible. The time had come for Bunny, who was so good with children, to start a family of his own.

There was, fortunately, an endless stream of things to be dealt with, which helped to divert my mother's attention from her deep-felt sorrow at the breakup. In October 1944 she was invited to the newly liberated Paris to investigate what help was needed, during which time she searched for and found Yola—alive and well, and living with Henri. To her amazement, on one of the tours of the city, she came across the street where, before the war, she used to get her shoes made. The little atelier was intact and she rushed in to see whether Monsieur Tetreau was still there. When the bell above the door jangled, the shoemaker looked up from the counter and a smile spread across his face. "Ah, Lady Louis!" he exclaimed. *"Vos souliers sont prêts!"*

Returning from France, she was offered an official posting

to SEAC as a representative of the Joint War Organisation. This was a most welcome prospect for my father, who had been trying to get her to join him for some time. After seeing in 1945 with us, my mother left and, once again, I was alone with Grandmama at her apartment in Kensington Palace.

Before returning to school that term, as I was now deemed old enough at fifteen to appreciate "serious" drama, I went twice to see Laurence Olivier in the film *Henry V* and was profoundly moved by his performance. The tale of a young king's coming-of-age and an army stranded on the brink of possible disaster in the face of a longtime enemy was a perfect metaphor for England at the time. When he spoke the words "We few, we happy few" the audience held their breath, each word echoing our national pride and resolve.

My mother wrote to tell us that she had traveled northeast through India to Burma. On the "leave train" from Calcutta she went third-class because she wished to experience firsthand what the conditions were like. It was very crowded, but being so slight, she managed to swing herself up onto the luggage rack, where she slept surprisingly well through the night. Patricia was also working hard, now a cipher officer in a secret underground establishment in Chatham. To her extreme embarrassment, a succession of scruffy young men kept turning up asking to see her. It turned out they were young Commandos on a training initiative test, each given ten shillings and sent off from the north of Scotland. They had to complete a number of tasks that took them all over the country. One was to obtain a naval handkerchief from a "Third Officer Mountbatten, Cipher, WRNS." No further clue was given. Several trainees seemed to find her very easily—although how they managed to penetrate the secret tunnel leading to the establishment without being shot was a mystery. Patricia gave the first handkerchief away gladly, as it was fun to be part of such a stealthy mission, but as she had to buy further handkerchiefs with her treasured clothing coupons, it soon became less amusing.

When the news came, in April 1945, that the Russians had attacked Berlin, I felt optimistic. Then, a few days later, Mussolini was captured and hanged by Italian partisans, and the situation began to spiral. Two days later, on 30 April, Hitler killed himself in his bunker, and then the Russians succeeded in taking Berlin. On 7 May the long-awaited news finally arrived—the Germans had surrendered. At last, for many, it was over. But not so for those of us with fathers and brothers in SEAC. On 8 May, as the streets resounded with joyous cries and all England celebrated victory in Europe, I lay in bed and thought of my father somewhere out in Asia. I had been blissfully unaware of the dangers he faced at the beginning of the war but now, at fifteen, kept up to date by our weekly war briefings at school, I knew much more and longed for his safe return.

I did have some good news for my father and I wrote to tell him that I had gained the highest marks in the school that year in the School Certificate examinations. His congratulatory telegram, "Expected nothing less," was somewhat disappointing, as I had longed to surprise him. Still, it was good to know he had such faith in me. I would soon have to change schools, and under the illusion that it was a finishing school that would equip me with the necessary skills for adult life, my mother opted for Hatherop Castle School in Gloucestershire, a rather beautiful old manor house set in sumptuous grounds that had only recently been derequisitioned.

Life was still fairly contained. I studied hard, attended early-morning Communion, waded loyally through my father's SEAC dispatches, and looked forward to concerts and plays during the school holidays. I hadn't yet been in love, much less experienced infatuation or heartbreak. I was shy, so while other girls at school were looking forward to "coming out" with great excitement, I was horrified at the thought of having to stand in a room full of hundreds of people I didn't know, sipping cocktails and trying to make polite conversation. I wasn't even that familiar with the "coming out" process as the war had put a stop to the parties.

While those fortunate people whose fathers and brothers had survived the war were now reunited, my family were still absent, dealing with the aftermath. My father took the surrender of the Japanese in Singapore. His priority was the repatriation of the British troops in Japanese prisoner-of-war camps. They were living in appalling conditions, many near death, and he needed someone to assess the situation for him. The person he felt most capable of doing so was my mother, so he sent her off with an Indian officer and a First Aid Nursing Yeomanry (FANY) woman assistant. They embarked on an incredible journey that included sleeping in the jungle, searching for unmarked camps that were rumored to be holding many prisoners. As the British had not yet reached these camps, she had to be escorted by fully armed Japanese soldiers, but she managed to gain their respect and none disobeyed her. She flew back with the vital information my father needed and the Far East Prisoners of War (FEPOWs) were lastingly grateful to her and to my family down the years—not to mention how proud my father was of the remarkable job she had done.

Patricia was at our father's headquarters in Ceylon with the WRNS, and I was in Gloucestershire, far away from them all. The only small consolation of having them all out in SEAC was that I had a gunboat on the River Irrawaddy in Burma named after me. Indeed, I was very impressed to be told that HMS *Pamela* (and its sister vessel HMS *Oona*, named after General Slim's daughter, who had just joined me at Hatherop) had even seen action in battle. Patricia's line in a letter to our father made me laugh. "How young," she wrote, "does a girl have to *be* exactly to have a boat named after them?"

Finally and thankfully—I was hardly able to contain my relief—everyone came home for the Allied Victory Parade and the parties and thanksgiving ceremonies. The first event took place in the sumptuously grand Buckingham Palace, followed by a terrifying list of social engagements as my parents caught up with their old friends. I was very pleased to see Bunny and Gina and to meet their new baby, Sasha. On the day of the parade itself, we gathered at the palace and were driven to the specially constructed saluting base in the Mall to watch the Victory Parade. We had been told that the whole route of the procession had been lined with hoardings to hide the bomb sites, but the crowd was so thick and animated that you wouldn't have been able to see them anyway. My mother, Patricia, and I took our seats moments before Winston Churchill and Clement Attlee arrived to a tumultuous reception from the crowd. When the king and queen and the princesses drew up in the state landau, the crowd went wild with cheering.

The parade was magnificent and must have taken weeks to plan. It began as two separate parades: a march-past of over twenty-one thousand fighting men and women from all the Allied countries and a display of all the types of machines that had helped them to victory. At the Houses of Parliament both parades came together to pass the saluting base as one impressive and continuous column. Field Marshal Sir

Bernard Montgomery—or Monty as he was affectionately known—was the first to pass before the king and queen, a small solitary figure standing sideways to attention in his jeep. His vehicle was closely followed by the chiefs of staff's procession that included my father and the other supreme allied commanders. They all saluted and my father, as he passed the saluting base, looked back at us and clasped his hands together in victory. His broad smile said it all: "We did it!" Later that evening, the royal family traveled down the Thames in the royal barge to the Palace of Westminster, with the crowds cheering from the riverbanks. The clever lighting of landmarks combined with a vibrant firework display made it seem as if the whole of London was aglow with pride.

There followed a number of parties, and as I had just passed my driving test—I had taken well to driving—I took the opportunity to give my parents a lift to Hampton Court, to a party hosted by the new Labour government. My father, as always, appeared in uniform, but my mother, warming to the "postwar" theme, assumed that others would be dressed to party. She chose an elegant long evening dress and a bright pink ostrich-feather fan, but on arrival, she realized that this was Austerity Britain and that the other guests were dressed in lounge suits or uniform and the ladies in short dresses. She looked around in panic, shoved the feathers into my father's hands, hissed, "Dickie, go and get rid of this," then promptly disappeared. She returned looking calm, her long dress tucked and twisted into a rather effective shorter dress. My father stood in the queue for the gents' cloakroom, face like thunder, clutching the ostrich-feather fan, wishing, for that moment at least, that his wife were a little more conventional.

In the following weeks and months, honors for my father flooded in. Among many accolades, he received honorary degrees from Oxford and Cambridge and was made a viscount. This meant that my sister and I became "Honourables," something that caused us both great embarrassment. One special honor was conferred on my father by the town of Romsey when he was granted the Freedom of the Borough— the first-ever such grant in their 339-year history. We all processed through the town with great ceremony and cheering and my father presented the mayor with a Japanese gun. He had given them prior warning and the councillors planned to mount it on the wall of the town hall. Plans had to be hurriedly changed when an enormous field gun weighing several hundred pounds arrived a few days before the ceremony and proved not at all suitable for mounting on anything other than a very strong outdoor plinth.

Meanwhile, Patricia had fallen in love. John Brabourne was my father's ADC and, somewhat romantically, they had met in Ceylon. Soon after they returned to England she finally agreed to accept his constant proposals of marriage. When she telephoned me at school, I experienced the weirdest sensation: I felt simultaneously more excited yet more despairing than I had ever been. I couldn't believe that I was losing my sister just when I thought my family had been reunited. But of course my elated misery didn't last for long. John could not have been nicer or kinder and it wasn't long before I began to adore him as the brother I never had. It certainly couldn't have been easy, coming into our family, especially when Grandmama was in argumentative spirit or introduced the names of various relations, both alive and long dead, to assist the chronology of her stories. One day she was recounting an anecdote (as well as interjecting in several other conversations around the table) and added, "That was when Willie came over from Bonn." Poor John was baffled, so he whispered urgently to Patricia, "Who is Willie?" To which she replied "Why, the kaiser, of course."

I got involved in the preparations for Patricia and John's wedding, which was to take place at Broadlands, even though the house was still mostly given over to the hospital. I was to be "head bridesmaid," but as the other three were princesses, the role of chief was really only titular and I felt shy telling the others what to do. My most important job was to keep a list of all the presents as they arrived and lay them out the day before the wedding for the guests to enjoy. There were gifts of jewelry, so after much debate my parents decided to hire a private guard that night—without telling me. As I was madly unpacking things at midnight, he burst in, pointing a loaded revolver at me. After we had both collected ourselves it was difficult to work out who was the more shamefaced, the guard for nearly shooting his employer's daughter or me for having been caught flapping around in my nightdress.

Patricia and John were married on 26 October, an unusually wet day, the weather, according to superstition, apparently indicative of a long and happy union. Romsey was beside itself with excitement for the "big wedding," buildings covered in bunting and people crowded along the route to the abbey. Some of the crowd had been waiting for up to ten hours in the pouring rain or had spent the night outside the abbey. Motor coaches had brought people from Shrewsbury, one hundred miles away, and Bournemouth, Salisbury, Winchester, and Southampton, one coach displaying a large notice: "Come and see the Mountbatten wedding. 8/6 Return."

The princesses and I had to wade unceremoniously through the streets of Romsey, holding our skirts up above the puddles while we walked with the king, the queen, our mother, and Cousin Philip. When we reached the door of the abbey, Princess Elizabeth turned to Philip and he casually reached behind Princess Margaret and took her coat. This small act jump-started a media frenzy as the press realized that it had glimpsed, however fleetingly, an air of ease and understanding between the pair. Newsreels confirmed the rumor, and royal gossip went into overdrive.

The abbey was filled to overflowing, and the gray stone interior with its Norman arches looked spectacular. The columns lining the aisles were silhouetted black against the light streaming through the stained-glass windows. Patricia was radiant in a dress of gold Indian brocade, with long medieval sleeves, a figure-hugging bodice, and a long fan-shaped train. She wore a beautiful combination of veils—one of tulle that my mother had worn and the other of lace belonging to the Brabourne family, through which glistened the diamonds and pearls of the tiara Grandmama had worn at the Russian court. Patricia shone amid the restrained utility clothing and uniforms of the congregation. In our dresses the color of forget-me-nots, we bridesmaids walked behind, our long skirts falling into folds, with Alexandra, the smallest, in front, followed by Princess Margaret and then Princess Elizabeth and myself as a pair behind her. John stood waiting with his best man at the end of the narrow aisle facing the Archbishop of Canterbury. Our father's beaming face clearly showed his pride as Patricia came up the aisle on his arm.

Back at Broadlands, I had difficulty in recognizing anyone, having removed my glasses for the day. When I bumped into the archbishop, he told me not to worry and reassured me he had been "a fine rugger player," and I was shocked on turning to see Miss Faunce bearing down on me, as it meant the person I had been speaking to earlier had not been my old headmistress at all. It seemed I wasn't the only one who was having difficulty adjusting to Patricia's newly married status either. With a roomful of guests to attend to, including the royal family, my father was somewhat alarmed—and touched—to find our butler Frank crying on the stairs, shaking his head in disbelief and repeating, "How can Miss Patricia leave a lovely home like this . . . ?"

It was a wrench having to return to school, especially when I received a call telling me that Lottie had died. She had been my most faithful companion throughout my childhood, and as I put the phone down, I could vividly picture myself in Malta bursting with joy as Yola gave her to me. I had to go to my bedroom after every lesson to cry, such was my distress. I realized I couldn't go on weeping for the rest of the term, however, so I consoled myself with the lines from *Antony and Cleopatra*: "Unarm, Eros, the long day's task is done, / And we must sleep," and got on with things as best as I could.

Then came a massive decision. Returning to Broadlands for Christmas in 1946, I learned that my father had been offered a new job. A huge weight hung over my parents, a heaviness that affected all of us as we left for a much-awaited and eagerly anticipated family skiing holiday in Switzerland. For this was no ordinary job. As an admirer of my father's achievements in SEAC, his ability to get on with people, his liberal sentiments, and because he was the king-emperor's cousin, the prime minister, Clement Attlee, wished my father to succeed Lord Wavell as the viceroy of India and oversee the transfer of power to an independent Indian government. The process was to begin as soon as possible and be over by June 1948. This offer had taken my father by surprise. For a start, in contrast to all the previous incumbents, my father was a naval officer, and among his many reservations he believed that if he took this role, it would mean the end of his naval career. But this was not his only worry. The command to divest England of the last jewel in the Empire, garnered under his great-grandmother, was not an easy one to accept. India was racked with political troubles and many more-experienced people before him had failed to forge a path to independence. He was also concerned and distressed that—despite his protestations—the Labour government had not told Lord Wavell of their intentions.

On 1 January 1947, just a few days into our holiday, my father was recalled by the PM, so he and my mother returned home, leaving Patricia, John, and me behind to finish a rather gloomy New Year holiday. There followed weeks of negotiation and stipulations—my father threw in some strong provisos, including the use of his old aircraft, a York, which he had flown in Southeast Asia, and a commitment from the Admiralty that he might return to the navy when the job was over. Most importantly, he asked that he be allowed to act on his own initiative and not have to refer every decision back to Whitehall. When it looked as though the prime minister and the cabinet might accept these stipulations, my father went to see the king. "Bertie," he said, "they are sending me out to do an almost impossible job. Think how badly it will reflect on the family if I fail." The king replied, "Think how well it will reflect on the family if you succeed," and told him he must go.

Back at Broadlands, my father took me for a ride, and as our horses plodded along he revealed that the proposed job was more than likely to come off and so I should not go back to school but instead go with my parents to India. He explained that while he and my mother fulfilled their roles as viceroy and vicereine, I could be useful helping with the entertaining and getting to know the student leaders who had just been released from jail. He talked and we rode for a very long time and as we came down Telegraph Hill, my head was spinning. I knew that my going with them was inevitable, and that even though there was still much to be resolved, my life was going to take a very different turn from this moment on.

For the next few weeks, I was in limbo and while pleased not to be going back to a girls' boarding school I was also apprehensive of being thrown into a completely new world. I had never mixed with university students, much less in an intensely political environment, and I knew next to nothing about India. While we waited anxiously for Parliament's decision, I spent my time with Grandmama, reading aloud to her since her eyes were becoming weak and she was distraught at having to give up reading, which was still her greatest pleasure. She might have fared better if we had had strong electric lighting, but because of the coal crisis, all the lamps glowed weakly, or were cut off altogether by the endless power cuts. To add to the collective misery, it snowed for eight weeks in a row, and one night in January was the coldest on record.

At last, in the middle of February, my father's appointment came through. Patricia, John, and I went to the House of Commons to hear the statement read. When the prime minister announced that Viscount Mountbatten was to become the viceroy of India with almost immediate effect, the House descended into chaos. Churchill, now in the Opposition, demanded to know why Wavell was being recalled. The debate was passionate and heated, but when we left Parliament, my father's appointment had been approved, and I knew for certain that my life was never going to be the same again.

There were only four weeks in which to prepare for our

departure. My mother and I needed suitable clothing, dresses fit for a vicereine and her daughter. We fumbled around the shops, which, because of the power cuts, were often in complete darkness, save for the odd candle. When we finally uncovered some lovely material, our lack of coupons—even with the small extra allocation we had been given—and the horrifying prices made it impossible to arrange anything like a suitable number of dresses. In the end my mother managed to buy a "gala" dress for the swearing-in ceremony and some fabric that her French dressmaker turned into pretty dresses. It was a treat for me to have anything new, so I was delighted by my new acquisitions.

I did what I could to prepare myself. India was already a familiar place for my father, as he had set up his Southeast Asia headquarters in New Delhi when he first took up his job as supreme allied commander. He gave me an elementary Urdu primer that had been published for army cadets several years before and I did my best to study it. My mother arranged for a Miss Lankaster, who had worked for the All India Women's Conference, to come and talk to me about the various student leaders I should meet. Being seventeen and pulled straight out of an English boarding school, I wondered just how far out of my depth I would be, how on earth I was going to be of any help at all in such a profoundly diverse and divided country, a country on the brink of such massive political and social change.

But there wasn't much time for reflection. Patricia announced that she was pregnant, and celebrating her good news proved a welcome diversion. My parents and I were summoned for tea at Marlborough House with Queen Mary, who sat so upright everyone felt compelled to do the same. Wearing a turban and enormous diamonds, she listened with great interest as my father explained what his role was to be, adding that Grandmama strongly disapproved of the politicians sending him out to do their dirty work. Queen Mary laughed delightedly at this. "Oh, dear Victoria," she said. "Ever the bluestocking. And never afraid to say what she thinks." My father smiled—we were all very proud of my grandmother's reputation.

The last ten days passed in a blur: updates from my father's viceregal staff on the growing unrest and political disagreements he was going to encounter on arrival in India; a visit on behalf of the king from the Duke of Gloucester to invest my father with the Order of the Star of India and the Grand Cross of the Indian Empire (a heart-stopping moment—on arrival, he realized that the decorations had been left on the backseat of the taxi. Luckily they were retrieved); a farewell cocktail party for over seven hundred people at the RAC Club, then a good-bye dinner with Patricia, John, and Cousin Philip, during which Philip told us that he had renounced his titles and become a naturalized British citizen, another P. Mountbatten to add to the confusion.

At last, on 20 March 1947, my parents and I drove down to Northolt in a royal car bulging with bodies, bags, and dogs, closely followed by a bunch of well-wishers. We posed for the press in front of the old York aircraft, and as the flashlights popped and I looked over to my waving sister, I thought back to the photographers at LaGuardia when I had left New York and how all that now seemed like a lifetime ago.

## 9

The cabin of the York was not pressurized, and as the plane bucked and fell among the air pockets, I was dreadfully sick. When we landed in Delhi, my first impression was of heat and haze. I had only a few moments to pull myself together, put on my hat and gloves, and hope that I looked presentable for the waiting photographers. My parents left the plane first and I followed, reeling slightly into the heat and wondering if I should risk making my white gloves grubby by wiping the dust off my face before I shook hands with the great many people awaiting us.

I went ahead with the staff in the cars and as we arrived at Viceroy's House, the sight of the dismounted members of the bodyguard on each of the wide imposing steps took my breath away. They were all Sikhs, tall, handsome, bearded men, resplendent in their black-and-gold turbans, scarlet uniforms with white breeches, and shiny black thigh boots. I curtsied to Lord and Lady Wavell and was introduced to their daughter Felicity, then watched as my parents arrived in a state landau escorted by the mounted viceregal bodyguard.

As was traditional, we had only one evening with the Wavells before they departed. I could do little but listen as Felicity brought me all her files, then began: "The Viceroy's

House compound houses five hundred and fifty-five domestic servants, drivers, gardeners, electricians, and grooms together with their families, so the compound holds around five thousand in total and we have a school and you will have to be the chief visitor for the school. And there is a clinic . . ." Furthermore, I was to succeed Felicity as the president of the Lady Noyce School for the Deaf and Dumb, which taught about seventy children aged between six and eighteen, who, without the protection of the school, would be unwanted and helpless. More files were banged down in front of me. It transpired that Felicity also worked part-time at a canteen for the Allied forces. "But," she said, "that's all fairly straightforward, so I'm sure you can work that one out for yourself." I could only smile politely. Felicity, in her twenties and recently married, seemed well equipped to cope with all these responsibilities, but I wasn't sure about any of it. Fresh out of school, not yet eighteen, with no training or skills beyond typing and speedwriting, I felt somewhat out of my depth. And she hadn't even mentioned all the student leaders who were about to be released from prison whom my father wanted me to contact.

India was on high alert, tense and fractious. The tragic violence of three days of rioting that followed Direct Action Day on 16 August 1946 had left over twenty thousand dead on the streets of Calcutta, Muslim and Hindu alike. The background was complex. India had long wanted self-government. Ever since British rule had weakened during the First World War, and following his return from South Africa, Mahatma Gandhi had convinced much of the population to push for independence through nonviolent disobedience, which had, until now, been very effective. The Muslim League had been agitating for a sovereign state for all Muslims—to be called Pakistan—since 1933. The British had been loath to lose India, but during the Second World War they had been forced to go begging to the country for help. In 1942 Sir Stafford Cripps had been sent with an offer to Gandhi: Britain would grant India the status of a self-governing dominion after the war if India were to support the Allied effort. Gandhi had refused—it was immediate independence or nothing—and stalemate ensued. Meanwhile, his Quit India Campaign was gaining momentum, and with India's rising expectations came mounting tensions, culminating in the riots, following which Mr. Jinnah, the leader of the Muslim League, strengthened his calls for the creation of Pakistan. Churchill had forbidden Lord Wavell even to talk to Gandhi, so his influence had been severely limited. After the riots, Attlee decided that independence could no longer be postponed but he needed a new viceroy to see it through. According to the prime minister, my father was the right man: "an extremely lively, exciting personality" with "an extraordinary faculty for getting on with all kinds of people . . . blessed with a very unusual wife."

So, unlike any other incoming viceregal family, we were not there to uphold the laws and traditions of the Empire but to dismantle them. The swearing-in ceremony was short but impressive. It took place in the Durbar Hall, and my parents processed in to the flash of photographers' bulbs as if they were film stars—which they could have been as they looked so handsome together, my father in white full-dress naval uniform and my mother in a long slim white dress. The new viceroy and vicereine took their places on the thrones but immediately seemed to be dwarfed by the surrounding pageantry and architecture. I sat watching, amazed to think that only four days before we had been bustling about the freezing, gray streets of a postwar London in the grip of austerity. I recalled Yola's story about my mother's encounter at a ball in the 1930s with a fortune-teller who told her, "One day you will be sitting on a throne, not an ordinary throne but a real throne nonetheless." At the time, my mother had dismissed this as "absolute bunkum."

The tour of our new home, Viceroy's House, took over two hours to complete. Our bedrooms and private sitting rooms were so far from the dining room that you had to allow ten minutes to get there. I soon realized that the house, Luytens's masterpiece, was like a hotel in which you might never see the other guests who were staying. In fact Patricia had warned me of this, as she had visited my father while he was staying there during the war. She had had great fun with the ADCs, and they had asked her whether she wanted to stay on for a bit. When she said that the viceroy hadn't invited her, they told her not to worry, he would never know.

But even if you were unlikely to come across other guests, you were never exactly alone, as there were so many servants milling around, with their precise tasks and roles. All the staff were male and all wore the headgear denoting their rank, as well as the viceroy's personal badge on their chests. I soon learned to distinguish among them: the bearers were the personal servants who wore dark blue in winter and white in summer, always with white turbans; *kitmagars* waited at table; *abdars* were the butlers and wine waiters (at dinner parties I loved to watch the head *abdar* raise his hands to either side of his turban as a signal for the serving of the meal to begin); the *chaprasis* ran messages and looked after the offices; the *syces* looked after our horses; the *dhobis* did the laundry; the Mughs from South India did the cooking; and I was surprised to discover there was a chicken cleaner who did nothing other than prepare chickens for cooking. Small boys in spotless white uniforms and caps acted as ball boys at the tennis courts and there was a whole team of drivers to service and chauffeur the viceregal cars. A position on the viceregal domestic staff ran in families and was highly prized, with periods of service ranging from fifteen to thirty-five years or more, and the service was faultless. My father, who would write himself memos and leave them on the floor of his study so that he would be sure to see them, was utterly thwarted by the efficiency of the servants, who would instantly throw away anything so untidy. Apart from a large number of outdoor gardeners there were twenty-five indoor gardeners to attend to the flower arrangements.

I had never had a lady's maid, let alone a man, to look after me, but I inherited Leela Nand, Felicity's bearer. When he said matter-of-factly, "Last lady much taller," my heart sank. But then he smiled and his eyes danced and I saw in that instant that there was hope for us. He was charming, as wrinkled and brown as a walnut, and it became clear as he bounded around the room with such energy and enthusiasm that walking was not an option for him. Everything he did was accompanied by giggles, sudden sulks, or even disturbing outbursts of tears. He wasn't always talkative, but when he did start, it would be a long while before he finished. My height was apparently not my only shortcoming. A couple of days later I was desperately searching for something that he had secreted in the most unlikely of places and he asked me whether I was going to box his ears. When I looked surprised and said, "No, of course not, Leela Nand," he seemed quite affronted. "Viceroy's daughter should," he said. After a few days, however, we began to understand each other, and within a few weeks, the delightful and ever-present Leela

Nand had become the most familiar element of my new life in India.

Leela Nand sewed beautifully and all my clothes were mended whether they needed to be or not. His special pride was darning. One morning he showed me the heel of a white tennis sock. I gazed at it with what I hoped passed for an expression of profound admiration, then I chose my words with care. "That's beautiful work, Leela Nand. It must have taken you hours to do." I paused, and then with mounting courage continued: "But don't you think it might have been better if you had used white cotton instead of red?" He looked at me, troubled by my stupidity, and said, very gently, "But no one could have seen it if I had done it in white."

They were all great characters. My father's Muslim bearer, Wahid Beg, was an avid reader. He had been taught to read English and he read everything there was to read, including the telephone directory. As this took a while, and my father often came into the room to find him sitting cross-legged on the floor, completely absorbed in a list of local names and addresses, Wahid Beg was always careful to put a marker in place before closing the book.

On the first evening after the Wavell party had left, my mother took me sightseeing to Humayun's tomb, a sixteenth-century red sandstone Mughal mausoleum. She pointed out how much things had changed since she had become engaged to my father at the Viceregal Lodge in 1922. In the intervening years, New Delhi had been designed and built together with Viceroy's House, where we now lived, eight miles from Old Delhi. The contrast between the widely spaced houses and government buildings, arches, and parks of New Delhi and the noise, color, and diversity of Old Delhi, crowded with bullock carts, holy cows, horse-drawn tongas, and thousands of bicycles that brought traffic to a near standstill, could not have been greater. For the first time too I was witnessing the vastly contrasting scales of poverty and wealth in this country—the grandeur of the viceroy's household somewhat alarming in its extravagance.

Before the onslaught of work began, my mother and I went to Tughlakabad, one of the seven cities of Delhi, then the Old Fort, and the Walled City, where we climbed to the top of Qutub Minar, the astonishingly tall red and buff sandstone tower. Our last stop was at the Jumping Wells, where, in return for some coins, boys jumped down sixty feet into a very shallow man-made pool. We succumbed to the little hands that pulled at us for annas but immediately wished we hadn't because they ran away laughing and somersaulting into the water below in such a cavalier fashion it was hard to believe the jump would not be fatal. Moments later, however, we were surrounded again and we beat a hasty retreat to the car.

The heat was fearful, and something I found great difficulty in getting used to. We had left the coldest English winter on record and within a few weeks found ourselves in the midst of the hottest weather Delhi had experienced for seventy-five years. We soon moved to the summer bedrooms on the north side of the house, as it was impossible to live permanently on the south side. The viceroy, family, and staff usually moved out to the cool hills of Simla during the summer, along with the rest of the British, but this year there was no time to lose, so we had to remain in the furnace.

My father and I soon established a routine of riding together every morning at 6:30 a.m. on the ridge above Delhi. On the first morning, when we arrived at the stables, an entire cavalcade of ADCs and police met us. We set off at a gallop and the ground was so rough and hard that I feared the horses would be lamed. After that, my father said he would take only two policemen and none of the ADCs. My mother seldom rode with us but on our return we ate breakfast together and then meetings began in earnest. My father's study was the epicenter of activity, his staff waiting for him to begin the day's work.

There were four aides-de-camp and they worked a duty rota: ADC1 was attached to "His Ex"; ADC2 was for "Her Ex" (a pretty cushy job until my mother came along); ADC3 looked after guests and the viceroy's daughter on special occasions; and ADC4 had a day off (until the pace of work became frantic). Their responsibilities were arduous and involved endless research, implementation of protocol, and organization of the diary. My father, a stickler for detail, made their lives even busier. At large luncheon or dinner parties, the ADCs were supposed to memorize the names and titles of the guests and present them to Their Exes. I admired how efficient they were at this—not at all easy when there were over one hundred people in the room. For lunches and dinners they had to ensure that the seating plan respected the order of precedence and the complex hierarchies of the princes, whose position in the rigid pecking order was marked by the number of guns' salute they should be accorded, twenty-one guns being the highest and nine the lowest. They worked in the "ADC Room," which invariably became the Cocktail Room at sundown, and they could also entertain their own guests in the Tiger Room. The men were all in their twenties, and the life and soul of any good party. To begin with, I was rather in awe of them and the glamorous young women who partied with them and whose hearts they frequently broke.

Before we had flown to India, my father had already worked out that if he was to hit the ground running, he would need to meet the four most important people behind the opposing political ideas and persuade them to cooperate with each other. This was his Operation Seduction; my father's charm offensive would give way to pragmatic strategies for movement and solution. And so it began, within a couple of days of arriving, with a visit from "the Father of the Nation," Mahatma Gandhi. The servants fell to the floor in ecstatic obeisance when they saw him, and a crowd of his followers remained outside the gates for the entire duration of his visit. I was thrilled to be introduced before the meeting began. I remembered the iconic photographs of him wearing his dhoti and sandals, surrounded by cheering mill workers, during his visit to Lancashire in 1931, but I was unprepared for how fragile he appeared just sixteen years later.

The visit was a success and many photographs were taken. As Gandhi was now so frail—and without one of his great-nieces, his usual "crutch"—he automatically put his hand on my mother's shoulder to steady himself as they crossed the threshold of my father's study. This delighted my mother and the photographers but sadly caused disgust and outrage when the photos were published in the British press. The general consensus seemed to be that his "black" Indian hand should not have been allowed to rest upon the "white" shoulder of the vicereine.

Gandhi had never before taken a meal at Viceroy's House, so it was an honor when he came back the next day, bringing with him his breakfast of goat's curds; it was a great concession for him to be seen eating with the viceroy. He offered some of the curds to my father, who politely tried to refuse, but Gandhi, with a mischievous smile, insisted. My father said later that it was the most unappetizing green porridge that he had ever tasted.

After Gandhi came his protégé, Jawaharlal Nehru, leader of the Congress Party. I had already heard about him from my parents, who had met him previously. In 1946 he had traveled to Malaya to meet the Indian community, and my father, the supreme allied commander at the time, had been warned by his staff that there might be trouble and that he should not meet Nehru. One of the staff had already refused to provide a car for him, and this so infuriated my father that he took Nehru in his official car to the YMCA in Singapore, where the meeting was being held. My mother was already there with a group of Indian welfare workers, and as she came forward to be introduced, a crowd of Nehru's admirers swarmed in behind him, knocking her off her feet. She crawled under the table, from where Nehru rescued her.

Given that Nehru's heroic rescue of her was one of her favorite stories, I was worried I might be disappointed by him in the flesh. But if anything, I was more impressed by him in real life—not only by his beautiful speaking voice and impeccable dress, a white buttoned-down tunic with the famous Nehru collar, jodhpurs, and a rosebud in his buttonhole, but also by his warmth and charm, which enveloped me from our first handshake. Watching him interact with others, I could see that he reacted to things instantly, was quick to laugh or make you laugh, and always interested in what you had to say. I realized that Gandhi and Nehru were the most extraordinary people I had ever met.

My father then met Sardar Vallabhbhai Patel, Nehru's colleague and also a disciple of Gandhi, who had worked with him in 1922 to organize civil disobedience, rising through the ranks to become a respected leader. He was the perfect antidote to Nehru's idealism, for when his colleague went off on a passionate tangent, Patel would remind him: "Don't go ahead of the people so far, come back to take them with you." He was tough and pragmatic but willing to listen, and my father formed a good working relationship with him. Not so with the icy and immovable Mr. Jinnah, president of the All-India Muslim League. Tensions between Hindus and Muslims were at breaking point, and not since the idea for a separate Muslim sovereign entity had been mooted had the situation been more acute. The violence following the recent Direct Action Day in August 1946 that had led to the deaths of more than twenty thousand Muslims and Hindus was the signal to Mr. Jinnah that India must either be divided or destroyed. He was an extremely sophisticated man, spoke perfect English, and was attired in an immaculate suit, as opposed to the other leaders, who wore national dress. At their very first meeting my father felt his charm offensive fail—something that had never happened to him before. Things got off to a bad start at the photo shoot. Mr. Jinnah had prepared a joke—assuming that my mother would be placed between the two men for the photo. When asked to pose he said, "Ah—a rose between two thorns." Unfortunately it was he who was placed in the middle of the composition.

As the day progressed, the going got tougher. I was not at the dinner at which my mother and father tried to get acquainted with Mr. Jinnah and his sister, Fatima, but their inability to crack the Quaid-e-Azam's (Great Leader's) hard exterior affected my father deeply, and he could talk of little else for days afterwards. It was obvious from the very first that Mr. Jinnah was going to make a smooth transition to independence impossible.

It became perfectly apparent once my father had met all four leaders, and taken on board their views, that there was no way they were going to be able to keep the peace while this impasse remained, and it was vital to transfer power as quickly as possible so that the various leaders could make their own decisions. He reasoned that if they were still in waiting nothing would be done because everything needed their approval, but if they were in power themselves, decisions could be taken more quickly.

At about this time, Lord Ismay, chief of the viceroy's staff, made his first presentation to my father. His message was hard to ignore: "The situation is everywhere electric . . . the mine may go up at any moment. If we do not make up our minds in the next two months . . . there will be pandemonium." When my father then convened a conference for the state governors, their diagnosis was the same. With the exception of Assam, all states reported that, in my father's words, "they were sitting on the edge of a volcano." They corroborated the Indian political leaders' view that the handover of power must happen as soon as possible. My mother organized her own miniconference with the governor's wives, as she hoped to take stock of their views and find out how they might help. She was taken aback to discover how little they knew about the situation.

The political meetings took place alongside the social occasions that my parents organized. Their insistence that the Viceroy's House should be seen as open and inclusive meant that we hosted two garden parties, three or four lunches for about thirty people, and two or three large dinners—at which my father insisted that half the guests must be Indian—each week. I was shocked as I overheard two guests say how "monstrous" it was that "all these filthy Indians" should have been invited, and when I told my father later, he was so incensed that he told the military secretary that if he ever heard anyone making a racist remark they should be asked to leave immediately.

As if the constant socializing at Viceroy's House wasn't enough of a whirlwind—new invitations arrived every day—there was a stream of cocktail parties for those going home. Though that wasn't always as clear as it might seem. On one occasion I set off for a good-bye party for the Scots Fusiliers, who, by the time I arrived, had been told they would be staying on. Pandit Nehru's gatherings were the most enjoyable. If the party was small, we would eat Indian food, though it took me a couple of tries to master the art of eating elegantly with my right hand. If it was large, there was often Indian dancing, sometimes a classical display, at other times one of the hundreds of different folk dances from around India.

I enjoyed meeting the Indian girls from Lady Irwin College. They were in their late teens, intelligent, amusing, and their conversation was thought-provoking. We would have great discussions about politics and religion, and though they were a mix of Muslims, Hindus, Sikhs, Buddhists, and Christians, we got along famously. We were all examining the beliefs we had been brought up with and, while their attitudes were inquiring, they were not combative and we had many impassioned debates. My parents had brought me up to be without prejudice and I was finally finding my voice. Through the friendship these girls offered, I realized that I was "coming out" in a way that would never have been possible as a debutante in London. I was delighted to celebrate my eighteenth birthday with them and other guests at a surprise party arranged by my parents at the palatial swimming pool. As I looked around at the white colonnades, my friends dancing beneath a sky full of stars, it felt so very far from the birthday a year before, which I'd spent alone at Broadlands with Grandmama.

It was not long before my mother turned her attention to the running of the house and the estate. Leaving no detail unexamined, she grilled the poor comptroller on management practice down to every last bit of expenditure. Within a week she had moved on to the servants' quarters, and by the end of April, she had been through everything. I accompanied her on many of her tours through the entire compound, including the stables, the primary school, and the dispensary, and I marveled at her ability to forge through the heat of the day, impervious to physical hardship. I wasn't as robust, and on one particular tour of the bodyguards' quarters I felt so faint after two hours in the harsh sun that to my great shame I had to sit down while my mother carried on. I was beginning to admire her more and more.

Now that my father and I had acquired new, well-mannered ponies and had cut our escort to two armed bodyguards, we could talk as we took our early-morning ride. And it became clear as we rode along the dirt track of the ridge, scattering the peacocks in our path, that I had now replaced my sister as my father's confidante. While this was purely the result of circumstance, my father, ever the extrovert, proceeded to share all his thoughts with me. As he did so, the significance of Bunny and Yola's place in my parents' lives became blindingly clear to me and I understood their situation with a new clarity. I felt so thankful that my father had resisted the temptation to divorce my mother and had kept the family together by including two people who brightened Patricia's and my own life.

Once I had found my feet and my mother and I had done all we could to reorganize the house, I started work in the Allied Forces Canteen, making milk shakes for the troops. It wasn't exactly difficult, although it took me a while to get to grips with the eight flavors and sometimes I felt we drank more than we sold. The canteen was meant to be for the Indian soldiers too, but in reality their pay was no match for the prices, so they tended to go elsewhere. I felt this was terribly unfair but didn't protest as I was told that they preferred to be served by Indian staff. As this job took up only two evenings a week, my mother sent me to see Lady Shone, the high commissioner's wife. She ran a clinic and dispensary in a huge tent outside Delhi for people from the surrounding villages. I would be most welcome in the mornings, Lady Shone said, beaming, as there was a permanent shortage of doctors and staff. And that was it. No more training or advice given; I would learn all I needed to know on the job. It was lucky that I had started Hindustani lessons with Mr. Krishnan Lal, though my spirits were dampened when he told me it would take a year to learn the grammar. By my calculation, I would just about be speaking the language when the time came to leave for home.

The tent opened my eyes to the poverty and need of the local people, and from the first moment I walked into the overpoweringly hot, dank clinic, I was overwhelmed by the work. Crowds of people queued outside from morning until night, and we saw everything from cuts and bruises to smallpox and TB. The more serious cases we had to send on to the Delhi hospital, but we managed to treat a wide range ourselves, many more than the hospital's outpatient departments. The male doctors were forbidden to examine Muslim women, so I would have to bury my head under their burkas and describe what I could see. There was no time to be shocked, though I found the riot-inflicted wounds made by the Sikhs' short curved swords—their kirpans—horrific. A less arduous task was to dole out pills and potions prescribed by the doctors. One small boy walked miles on a regular basis to collect pills for his family, and I worried that he didn't fully understand which were for what. Some of the young women were given colored-bead necklaces to demonstrate on which days of the month it was safe to have intercourse—a very elementary method of birth control. We were unsure of their effectiveness and suspected the necklaces ended up being worn as a pretty ornament.

By the end of April, the unrest in the northwest of India resulted in intense rioting, towns and villages in the Punjab and North-West Frontier Province (NWFP) being pillaged and burned down. Hindu and Sikh refugees were streaming out of the area, and my parents decided they needed to see the scale of the problem for themselves. We flew up to Peshawar on the border of India and Afghanistan to be met by the governor of the NWFP, Sir Olaf Caroe. He told my father that a large, angry crowd of between sixty and one hundred thousand Muslim League Pathans had assembled in the town to meet the viceroy with their demands. There was a rumor that they intended to kill him. Sir Olaf asked my parents not to go as he could not guarantee their safety, but they were not to be dissuaded—though I was firmly instructed to remain behind in Government House.

My parents went on ahead and climbed up the embankment of the railway to look down on the chanting mob of thousands. Then my father took my mother's hand and they picked their way over the steep rocky ground towards the crowd. Incredibly, the sight of a small white woman coming towards them—perhaps also because both my parents were wearing their jungle-green suits, green being the holy color of the Pathans—seemed to quell their anger. My father saluted the people and suddenly the cries of *"Pakistan Zindabad!"*

(Long live Pakistan!) subsided. He had succeeded in turning a crisis into an opportunity, much to the relief of the governor and his staff. And positive news of this turnaround must have traveled ahead, for the next day we were able to drive up the Khyber Pass to the Afghani frontier to attend a *jirga* of three hundred chiefs of the Afridi tribe. The drive was the most extraordinary of my life—wherever I looked on the skyline there were men on crags with rifles slung over their shoulders. My father said that the Afridis asked more pertinent and demanding questions of him than had been posed at any press conference.

On the third day of our trip, we flew to Rawalpindi in the Punjab and traveled on to survey the damage inflicted on the ransacked towns. Kahuta had been burned to the ground, and everyone we met told the most heartrending stories of internecine violence that stood comparison with any of the worst atrocities of the Second World War. My father wrote that the visit to Kahuta brought home the "magnitude of the horrors" of the unrest. This was one of only two trips that my father would be able to make to witness the problems at first hand before independence, but for my mother it was the first of many, and she would undertake such trips for the rest of her life. The next day she took me to visit the Sikh refugee camp at Wah, and I saw for myself what horrors and indignity the newly inflamed religious intolerance could do to former neighbors. Gangs of marauding Muslims had forcibly humiliated the Sikhs by shaving their heads, making them break one of their five sacred oaths. The weeping victims who fell to kiss my mother's feet when we arrived, begging for help and showing us their scarred heads, were among the most distressing things I had ever seen. Later, we were to be deluged with equally dreadful stories from displaced

Muslims, and I could see how people on each side were both victims and perpetrators.

By the beginning of May, my father felt he had seen enough. There could be no further delay to independence. He sent Lord Ismay back to London to deliver the "Mountbatten Plan" to the government. The brief hiatus after he left revealed the depths of my parents' exhaustion. It was only a little more than two months since my mother had undergone a partial hysterectomy and, since we had arrived in India, she had not stopped. Likewise, my father had been working seventeen-hour days for over six weeks. When and if the British government approved his plans for the handover of power, my parents were going to need all the energy they could muster to see them through. I was relieved and grateful when it was decided we should have a few days off in Simla before the onslaught began.

## 10

Being up in the cool hills of Simla, more than seven thousand feet above sea level, amid fragrant woods of pine and deodar, was both relaxing and reinvigorating, and while my mother thought the house "hideous, bogus English baronial. Hollywood's idea of a viceregal lodge," I found it rather appealing, with its beautiful lawns and extraordinary views. I could feel my lungs filling with clean, fresh air as I began to unwind from the last few frenetic weeks. Taking afternoon tea with my parents on the lawn in front of the stunning arched veranda, looking down through the verdant, lush woods, and watching little black monkeys jump across the trees made me realize how much I was enjoying this time in India with them.

Nothing better illustrated the complications of our new life than my father's conversation with Douglas Currie, his military secretary. When he had told him of his intention to take a short break at Viceregal Lodge the following week, Douglas held up his hands, saying that this would be "totally impossible to organize in less than a month." When my father replied that there would be only five in our party—he intended to invite Pandit Nehru and Krishna Menon to stay for a few days—and we would therefore need only a skeleton staff, Douglas had still looked perturbed. When my father then suggested that he just book us into a hotel to save any to-do, Douglas was so shocked that within a few hours the whole viceregal staff had gone into overdrive, rising to every challenge to enable the impossible to happen, the result of which was that now we were here, three people, waiting for two guests, attended by 180 servants. "If this is what Douglas calls a skeleton staff, then no wonder we are in a mess," remarked my father.

We settled into a routine: while my father attended to his papers during the day, my mother and I explored the surrounding hillsides, chatting as we walked, and then in the evening the three of us walked down into the town. My mother had banned us from taking the viceregal rickshaws after our first ride, regarding this as utterly degrading for the rickshaw coolies, and mortified at the idea of riding in a vehicle pulled by human beings. The viceregal coolies in their smart uniforms were bewildered. Once in town, we mingled with members of the British Colony, shopping along "the Mall," and most delightfully for me we went to a performance of the famous Simla Amateur Dramatic Club. It was a well-earned contrast from the whirl of our lives in Delhi.

After a few days Pandit Nehru arrived. He was such an interesting and amusing companion, so at ease with us and eager for us to be at ease with him, and like everyone else we were soon calling him Panditji. Soon afterwards Krishna Menon arrived. He was a long-standing friend of Pandit Nehru and acted as his special representative. He had also been Labour councillor for the London borough of St. Pancras for several years. The following day Panditji gave us a yoga demonstration, finishing with a flourish. "And this," he said, standing on his head and beaming at us upside down,

"is how I attempt to solve India's problems every morning."
Within seconds of being up the right way, he had all four of
us in different yoga positions on the floor. "You see, Pammy,"
he advised, "you will find that yoga is good for all manner
of things." I noticed that he used that phrase "all manner
of things" so much that it wasn't long before I nicknamed
him "AMOT," which didn't appear to irk Panditji. My father disapproved, however, so I dropped it. It was good to
get to know Krishna Menon better. He had kindly sent me a
copy of Nehru's book *The Discovery of India*, keen for me
to familiarize myself with Nehru's wisdom. Krishna looked
alarmingly like Mephistopheles and had that Indian way of
telling you exactly what he thought without, as the English
were apt to do, hiding his true feelings for the sake of manners. He and Nehru spent most of the small hours of the
night in furious political discussion.

In a flash, our time in the hills was over and my mother
flew off on a tour of inspection of the riot areas while my
father and I returned to Delhi, which felt like a furnace from
the moment we landed. The heat in the shade was 113°F, in
the sun anything up to 150°. But we returned to good news—
Lord Ismay's visit to London had yielded a positive response
and so, on my mother's return, my parents left for London
for discussions regarding my father's proposals. Meanwhile
the founder of the Caravan of India—a nondenominational,
nonpolitical youth organization actively involved in welfare
work—had asked me to open their summer bazaar and fun-
fair. While I was perfectly happy to be involved, I was ab-
solutely stiff with fear at the prospect of making my first
speech in public. When the day came, I arrived having had
little sleep and feeling hot and bothered in my white gloves
and little white hat. I took a deep breath, tried to conjure up

the most useful tips on public speaking from Miss Faunce, and launched into my speech. My mouth was dry and my heart was thumping, I forgot huge chunks of it, and I probably sounded a little too relieved as I hurtled to the end, but as soon as I said ". . . and so I pronounce this bazaar officially open," there was much kind applause. I looked at the encouraging faces around me as I cut the ribbon and breathed a sigh of relief: my first, most terrifying speaking engagement was over.

While my parents were in England, the senior governor, Sir John Colville, governor of Bombay, came to stand in for my father. He and his wife took me to a party given by Panditji. I was honored to find myself seated next to our host, and as he was keen to hear my experiences of India so far, I told him how much I had learned from his book. He asked me whether I had read his *Glimpses of World History* or the book of letters he had written for his daughter Indira when she was a child, but as they were both unobtainable, I had to say that I hadn't. A couple of days later a parcel arrived containing both books and a note: "Do not think that you must read through the 900-odd pages of the *History*, that is enough to depress any person. If and when you are in the mood for it, you can just dip in where you like." I was so touched and proud that he had thought to send the books to me.

My parents returned at the end of May, now proud grandparents. They told me that Lilibet and Cousin Philip were soon to announce their engagement and they were going to ask me to be a bridesmaid. But most importantly, they said that both Attlee's cabinet and Churchill's Opposition had approved the "Mountbatten Plan."

As the partition of India seemed inevitable, much to my father's regret his plan encompassed a divided India. He advocated an early transfer of power from British rule to two successor states, India and Pakistan. In so doing, he wanted Congress to approve dominion status so that India could remain in the Commonwealth for the sake of her economic strength and defense. The plan also proposed a referendum in the North-West Frontier Province to see whether its people wanted to join India or not, giving the princely states the option of joining either state or remaining independent, and the setting up of a boundary commission to determine the boundaries of the provinces of Assam, Punjab, and Bengal.

It was a major step in the right direction to have the British government's approval, but to implement the plan's recommendations, my father needed to get the agreement of the Indian leaders. We held our breath as their talks went on, behind closed doors. For two days, they debated, discussed, cajoled, and rationalized. From time to time someone would emerge looking dazed but determined, and as the reporters and photographers camped outside waiting for news, the tension built. Eventually, my father called for a consensus by midnight on 3 June. Only Mr. Jinnah held back, saying that he could not agree to the plan without first passing it before the Muslim League. My father finally got around this by asking him to at least nod his head to indicate that he would not delay the talks any longer even if he could not give his verbal agreement.

On 4 June, at the first press conference ever given by a viceroy, my father, speaking impressively and without notes, announced to the world's waiting media that, owing to complete and constant disagreement, it was not possible to forge ahead with plans for a united India, and as such dominion status would be granted for two self-governing states, India and Pakistan. You could see how surprised people were by his next statement: that the date for partition was set for 15 August, little more than two months away. The fourth of June happened to fall on Gandhiji's weekly day of silence, so he was not present, and there was great concern that he might not approve of the plan, especially as his disapproval could provoke a mass uprising. It was therefore a huge relief when, at his next prayer meeting, he announced that if "Hindu and Muslim cannot agree on anything else (aside from partition) then the viceroy is left with no choice." My father later wrote to my sister that 2–3 June had been the "worst twenty-four hours of my life."

But it wasn't over. Next my father had to gather his strength and explain the decision to another group of leaders—the rulers of the 565 princely states. These men, who had once been the most powerful in India, had seen their power decline dramatically during British rule, but nevertheless they still held sway over their people. The Chamber of Princes had been established by royal decree in 1920 as a forum in which the princes could discuss their needs or air their grievances with the British. Now, just over a quarter of a century later, they were about to be asked to relinquish much of their remaining power and to accede their state either to India or Pakistan in return for a modicum of independence. My father hoped that his friendship with several of them, established during his tour with the Prince of Wales in 1921, would help. But as he explained to me on one of our morning rides, asking the princes to choose between Hindu India and Muslim Pakistan was fraught with complexities, for in several cases the Indian ruler did not share the same religion as his people. Kashmir, for example, had a Hindu ruler but was mainly a Muslim state, and Hyderabad had a Muslim ruler but was mainly Hindu.

Some of these maharajas were astonishingly wealthy, notably the most senior prince in India, the Nizam of Hyderabad, who was, according to *Time* magazine, the richest man in the world in 1937. Accumulators of wealth, jewels, wives, and myths, these men gave rise to legends that were fantastic but often true. The Maharaja of Gwalior owned a fully functioning miniature train set made of solid silver—I later saw it for myself—that moved around his long dinner table, delivering port, brandy, and cigars to his guests. The Maharaja of Patiala created his own summer retreat to rival Simla after Lord Kitchener banned him from the hill station. Affronted, Patiala created a summer palace across the mountains at Chail, visible from Simla, and as he was cricket-obsessed, the maharaja went one step farther and built the highest pitch in the world.

The Mountbatten Plan was finally agreed to by most of the Indian princes, but the Maharaja of Jammu and Kashmir and the Nizam of Hyderabad would not make up their minds. Eager to smooth the way, Panditji, as a Kashmiri, decided he would visit the maharaja to see whether a personal intervention might help. But to bypass the danger of Nehru being humiliated should the maharaja not change his mind, my father accepted the prince's long-standing invitation, and we went to see him ourselves. This was an enjoyable, yet ultimately frustrating, trip. As guests, we had a busy and varied stay as the maharaja had laid on a fantastic sightseeing itinerary. We visited Nishat and from there were taken in his highness's luxurious *shikara* out on Lake Dal, its glassy waters reflecting the backdrop of the distant mountain range, one of the most beautiful sights I had ever seen. We were then sent to fish in a trout stream at Thricker for a whole day, returning to court to be lavishly entertained by the maharani and their son "Tiger." She showed us her astonishing collection of jewels and we were given delicious food. But in all this time there had been no sign whatsoever of the maharaja himself. We were told he had developed a severe bout of colic and his whole retinue tiptoed around the place in a state of nervous tension. For the five days of our visit there was never a chance for my father to discuss which way Kashmir was to accede.

We returned to the frenzy of Viceroy's House. My father had his famous calendar made and distributed about the offices, counting down the number of days to partition. Nothing was a foregone conclusion, however, as the arguing between Congress and the Muslim League continued, becoming so fierce that two separate cabinets had to be formed. And then bad news flooded in from the Punjab and Bengal, both states having voted for partition. The question of who was to allocate the boundaries of the two new dominions remained. The Muslim League requested that the UN should undertake this task but Congress would not agree. Instead, Sir Cyril Radcliffe, a law lord famous for his integrity, arrived from London. I was relieved that such a well-respected, impartial man had been appointed to this task as I was worried about how exhausted my father looked, how haggard and weary he seemed on our morning rides.

I continued with my work at the canteen and the clinic, learning Hindustani and taking care of Neola, a delightful little mongoose given to my father, who immediately passed him on to me. To my good fortune he was accepted by the servants, who did not, as a rule, like having pets around the place. Panditji told me that, in India, mongooses had proved popular companions in jail, something he had witnessed himself during his long years of incarceration as a political prisoner. When I said how awful that must have been, he said simply that it had allowed him precious time for reflection and writing, adding playfully, "It would do you some good, Pammy, to spend a little time in prison."

Neola, rather unimaginatively named since his name means mongoose in Hindustani, was proud and fierce and I fell in love with him. And while he reared up at every corner as if he were about to tackle a snake twice his size, and bit any man who tried to touch him, he accepted me. Within a few days I had trained him to ride on my shoulder as I walked about the house. My father didn't fare so well: despite my attempting to train Neola to use paper as a litter tray, he couldn't distinguish between scrap paper and the important papers on my father's desk, mysteriously preferring state documents. At breakfast Neola also seemed to prefer leaping onto my father's lap and, quick as a flash, stealing his eggs, leaving him holding his knife and fork above an empty plate and roaring, "Someone give that brute an egg of his own!"

Neola loved eating eggs, but whenever he tried to bite the shell, the egg often snapped out of his jaws and he became very frustrated. My father remembered from Rudyard Kipling's "Rikki-Tikki-Tavi" just what a mongoose is supposed to do—grip the egg in its front paws and with its back legs apart hurl it at a wall or hard surface, so that it shatters and can be eaten. So my father told me to hold Neola firmly and make him watch. He got down on the floor, opened his legs, and just as the egg hit the wall, a *chaprasi* came through the door, somewhat surprised to see His Excellency the Viceroy in such a position. Neola soon became known as the "Time Waster" owing to his inquisitive antics—I loved watching him rolling around in a wastepaper basket, knocking the telephone off the receiver, and listening to the operator asking endlessly "Number, please." If I was wearing my long evening dress with the floor-length sash, one of his favorite games was to launch himself at me as I was leaving the room, cling on to the length of satin using his teeth, then swing back and forth until the sash was untied. I would have to release myself, then dash down, late and disheveled, while my unrepentant mongoose tumbled around the room in delight.

Before Krishna Menon left to take up his recently appointed post as high commissioner to the UK, he took me to one of Gandhiji's prayer meetings. I had been keen to go for some time and promised to report back to my parents, who had been advised against going (though my mother had already had tea with him, the first vicereine ever to do so). We were to meet Gandhiji before prayers at his small quarters in Banghi Colony, where the poorest of the poor, "the Untouchables," lived. His room was tiny but neat and he greeted us from his usual cross-legged position on the floor. He beckoned me to join him in front of a low table and showed me one of his few remaining possessions—a small ivory carving of the Three Wise Monkeys. Then, with a twinkle, he said, "So, my friend, tell me all about the happy event." For a moment I was thrown, until I realized that he was referring to the news about the engagement of Philip and Princess Elizabeth that had been announced across the world that morning.

Then Gandhiji walked outside to a platform, aided by a great-niece on either side. I followed and sat behind him next to Krishna and Rajkumari Amrit Kaur, a Kapurthala princess and one of Gandhiji's long-serving secretaries. In front of us was a crowd of thousands who fell silent as soon as Gandhiji appeared on the raised dais. He read a verse from the Koran, we sang an Arabic hymn, followed by a Christian one, and then there was two minutes' silence. No one moved for the entire time. After this Gandhiji spoke in Hindi for forty minutes. Still no one moved. His discourse was spontaneous and unscripted, and as he spoke, Amrit Kaur wrote down every word. I watched the people listening to Gandhiji so intently and knew I was witnessing something extraordinary.

A few days later, I too benefited from his compassion, even though the reason was pretty insignificant. I was riding sidesaddle on a new horse when out with my parents on the ridge. When my horse shied suddenly, I was thrown to the ground and knocked unconscious. I was carried home bruised and concussed and had to remain in bed. Imagine my surprise and pleasure when I received a get-well message from Gandhiji, addressed to his "naughty friend."

On 25 July my father addressed the Chamber of Princes again and managed to persuade them all—with the exception of Kashmir and Hyderabad—to accede while he was still viceroy so that he could help protect them as best as he could. Things were now moving fast. My father told our favorite ADC, Sayed Ahsan, that, as a Muslim, he should go to Karachi to help set up Mr. Jinnah's Government House, and the adjutant of the bodyguard, Major Yacoub Khan, went too. We were very sad to have to say good-bye. As partition approached, Nehru appeared as exhausted as my parents, and I suggested he make a short visit home before the transfer of power. He wrote and thanked me for "the efficient arrangement" of his brief return to Allahabad and Lucknow, once again demonstrating his impeccable manners, taking time for such a kind gesture, especially during such a frantic period. It seemed he wasn't able to give his mind the complete rest it needed, however, for he wrote, "Last night I did something very unusual for me, I went to the cinema. I was very tired after a huge public meeting that I had addressed and suddenly decided to divert my mind to something else. The film was not exactly amusing: indeed it rather shook me up. It was all about the preparation of the atom bomb and the destruction of Hiroshima."

At last the day of independence arrived. Although 15 August had been chosen, Indian astrologers had immediately protested that this date was "inauspicious," and so it was decided to start the ceremonies at midnight on the fourteenth. That day, we flew to Karachi to be at the ceremony for the creation of the Dominion of Pakistan. My parents drove in an open car with the Jinnahs, while I followed behind with Begum Ra'ana Liaquat Ali Khan, the new prime minister's wife. The streets were thronged with ecstatic crowds, chanting their support, shouts of *"Quaid-e Azam Zindabad!"* and *"Mountbatten Zindabad!"* resonating for miles. Intelligence had warned before the ceremony that a bomb might be thrown during the procession but luckily everyone returned to Government House unharmed. In a rare show of emotion, Mr. Jinnah leant across and, smiling, put his hand on my father's knee. "Your Excellency," he said, "I'm so glad to get you back safely." As we flew back to Delhi my father told me how he had forced himself not to give voice to his thoughts: "If only you knew the efforts I have gone to for the last several weeks to preserve *your* safety."

A few hours before the Indian independence ceremonies were due to begin, Panditji and Rajendra Prasad, the president of the Congress Party, came formally to invite my father to take up the post of constitutional governor-general of India, representing the British sovereign—a ceremonial position, with day-to-day power resting in the hands of the Indian cabinet. They presented him with an envelope which, they informed him, contained a list of everyone in the new government. You can imagine my father's surprise when he opened it to find that a blank piece of paper had been put in there by mistake. During dinner at Viceroy's House, we raised our glasses for the last time to toast the king-emperor and the viceroy. Then, just before midnight, we turned on the wireless and listened to Panditji's wonderfully moving speech to the new nation: "At the stroke of the midnight hour when the world sleeps, India will awaken to life and freedom."

Friday, 15 August 1947 was one of the most incredible days in history. I have never experienced such an outpouring of excitement and joy. The noise of crowds cheering rang throughout India and the expressions of respect and admiration for my parents from both the new government and the Indian people were remarkable.

For us, Independence Day began with my father being sworn in as governor-general while the new Indian flag was hoisted over what was now Governor-General's House. In the Durbar Hall, it was pure theater as the golden thrones with their sumptuous red velvet canopies were spotlit, reflecting the gold of the carpet, and bathing the room in a warm glow. My mother looked marvelous in a long gold lamé dress with a little wreath of gold leaves on her head, and my father was resplendent in his white full-dress naval uniform with the blue ribbon of the Garter and his other decorations. The trumpeters in scarlet and gold heralded a splendid entrance, and as the doors were thrown open everyone sang "God Save the King" followed by the new Indian national anthem, "Jana Gana Mana." Then my parents were driven off in the state landau to the Constituent Assembly. There were so many people surrounding the Council House, however, cheering *"Jai Hind,"* that the state carriage was engulfed and Nehru and the other government leaders had to come out to calm the crowd and create a passage for my parents to get to the hall.

Once inside, my father read out a message from the king and made his own speech, which resulted in prolonged and joyous cheering. Then the president of the Assembly, Rajendra Prasad, read out messages of congratulations and good wishes from other countries and gave an address that concluded by paying tribute to my parents. Again, making their way outside was impossible, as the crowds had pressed so tightly against the doors, and it took several minutes even to leave the chamber. Once out in the bright sunlight, we watched as the crowds clapped and shouted themselves hoarse with cries of *"Pandit Mountbatten, ki jai!" "Lady Mountbatten! Jai Hind!"* as well as similar exclamations to all the Indian leaders. There were even some cries of "Mountbatten Miss Sahib!" or "Miss Pamela," or they just chanted *"Angrezi! Angrezi!"* I hurried to get back into the car and went ahead of my parents' procession to Prince's Park for the flag salutation ceremony.

A tsunami of people filled every possible bit of space as far as the eye could see. We climbed out of the car and attempted unsuccessfully to fight our way on foot towards a low platform surrounding the flagstaff. My parents had said that this would be India's day and you could see it on every single face, hear it in every voice. It struck me as odd that there were babies up in the air, high above heads, until I realized that their parents simply had to thrust them up above the crowds to avoid their being crushed. The bicycle being passed above everyone's heads appeared surreal but the crowd took it good-naturedly—there just wasn't a single inch of space in which to put it down.

We were about thirty yards away from the grandstand, feeling helpless, until Panditji made his way over to us, walking on people's laps and having to steady himself by grabbing the nearest shoulder. "Come on, Pammy," he yelled above the din. He reached out for me to grab his hand. "But I can't walk over people," I shouted feebly. "Of course you can! Nobody will mind. Come on!" He waved his hands. I looked at Panditji's feet—he was wearing flat leather sandals. I was wearing high-heeled shoes. "Take your shoes off!" he shouted. Then he pulled me up and over hundreds of human laps while everyone laughed and cheered us on. When we reached the flagstaff, he told me and Maniben Patel, Vallabhbhai's diminutive daughter, to stand with our backs to the pole so that we would not be knocked over in all the excitement, and from this spot we had the perfect view of the exuberant chaos.

The state carriage finally crept into view, but neither it nor the bodyguard escort could come any closer without running people over. Eventually, my father stood up in the landau and saluted the flag. Panditji struggled over to them but this time it proved impossible to clear a passage for them. In his attempt to help, Panditji came so close to being crushed that my father hauled him onto the carriage hood, much to the delight of the crowd. He then rescued several women and children from being crushed by the horses' hooves until, in addition to the uniformed attendant standing on the back, there were ten more people in the carriage along with my parents, with the new prime minister riding triumphantly on top.

That night we gave a dinner party for over one hundred

people, and after dessert we all wandered out into the blissful cool of the night to watch the illuminations and fireworks
from the magically lit Mughal Gardens. This was followed
by a reception for two and a half thousand people—each one
of whom was presented to my parents. The atmosphere was
intoxicating, but eventually I had to go to bed, exhausted but
exhilarated. The next day my mother and I went to see the
prime minister raise the new dominion flag over the Red Fort
in Old Delhi. In the midst of this dramatic setting, and with
the sound of eight hundred thousand people cheering and
singing, my father spoke. India, he said, should be allowed to
have the "joy of Independence Day" before it faced the misery of partition. They were prescient words. But for now, the
joy lingered. My father's plan had been fulfilled. India was
now an independent country. It was extraordinary to think
that I had witnessed the birth of two new nations and been
present while history was in the making.

## ~ 11 ~

After all the ceremonies and parties we next flew to Bombay. This was my chance to meet the student leaders who, following independence, had been released from prison. They had previously been involved in protests, agitating for the end of British rule in India. I sat in my sitting room in Government House, waiting for my guests, tea at the ready. I was impressed that their leader, Dinkar Sakrikar, whose name had been given to me by Miss Lankaster, had accepted my invitation, and I wondered whether, if I had been imprisoned for my beliefs, I should have been willing to go to a meeting at the official residence of the government that had imprisoned me. I had a long time to think, and worry, about this because twenty minutes after our appointed time, there was still no sign of my guests. I called the ADC room only to discover, to my absolute horror, that the police sentries had detained the students. These police happened to be the very same men who had arrested the students before they were sent to prison, however, and both groups had whiled away the time reminiscing, until the ADCs rang through and approved their entry.

Although I was better acclimatized and much more knowledgeable about Indian politics than I had been when my father first brokered the idea of my interacting with the students, I was nevertheless nervous that I might be faced with a disgruntled, confrontational group of former dissidents, and now it was about to happen, I was even more concerned. But I need not have worried one bit for I was met with smiling faces and much laughter about what had happened, and we talked easily over tea. Early the next morning we set off to see the institutions where they studied—the G. S. Medical College, Bombay University, and the J. J. School of Art. They drove me in a car flying the new Indian flag and introduced me to many of their friends. We rushed around excitedly, and it was fascinating, but there was not really time to talk as I had to be back at Government House to fly off with my parents at noon. I arrived back dripping with bouquets, garlands, and presents, overcome by my welcome and their friendliness.

Back in Delhi, it wasn't long before news came in that the now-divided Punjab was in total crisis. My mother set off at once with Rajkumari Amrit Kaur—Gandhiji's personal secretary had now become the new minister for health—to survey the region for herself. They found horrific scenes and mass hysteria, "the place of the dead," as Muriel Watson, her personal assistant, described it to Panditji and my father on their return. But of course it didn't end there. In the coming weeks my mother flew from one region to another, witnessing the atrocities at first hand. There were times when the reports were so terrible that I feared for her safety and even her life.

Millions of refugees were moving in opposite directions using the same roads. When a Hindu or Sikh had had his village burned and his family massacred by Muslims, or vice versa, they would be overcome by blind rage when they saw people they now considered to be their mortal enemies on the opposite side of the road. They would attack, then their inflamed coreligionists would join in, so fighting would break out among those who had previously been fleeing to safety. It was heartbreaking to think that for many years these people had lived peacefully as neighbors.

Not afraid of facing the crisis head-on, my mother kept Panditji and Rajkumari informed of the terrible situation in the ever-expanding refugee camps. At one Muslim camp, she and her team intervened when they found a gang of Hindus and Sikhs trying to set fire to it and burn the inmates to death. The ADCs who traveled with her were amazed at her bravery and often found that she took them into situations that even they, as serving officers, were alarmed by. One of her major concerns was the abduction of Hindu and Sikh women in Bengal. There were hundreds of cases of women being raped and forced to become Muslim. My mother's office went into overdrive, helped by the presence of the feisty, angry Punjabi refugee Jaya Dalip Singh, the niece of Rajkumari.

Jaya was very bitter when she arrived, having come to Delhi with her wealthy family after they and their entire community lost their homes in Lucknow. Jaya, who was twenty-one, was initially in shock, her life having collapsed overnight. On arrival in Delhi she had turned her back on her family, spending her evenings in nightclubs, living what she termed "a fast and loose life." In despair, her parents appealed to Rajkumari for help. "Send her to my friend Lady Mountbatten," Rajkumari told them. "She needs someone who can speak Punjabi when she visits the refugee camps. She will sort Jaya out." Jaya's fate was sealed.

I liked Jaya, her energy and her plight touched me, and here, at last, was someone nearer my own age. She certainly needed someone to off-load her frustrations onto and I was a willing listener. She had witnessed atrocities firsthand and now possessed a wisdom that came from direct experience; while I was acutely aware of the problems that fueled the country's burgeoning crisis, I had been sheltered from the worst of it and would be unlikely ever to suffer in the way she had. Jaya was proud to be from the Punjab, having always considered herself Punjabi before Indian, and she was furious with my father because in all the discussions about independence, the countless meetings of committees and councils, no Punjabi representative had been in attendance, and therefore their land and their lives had been forfeited. "Congress believes that I should be happy that the Punjab has been sacrificed for the 'freedom of India,'" an impassioned Jaya told me. "Well, I am not!"

Jaya came to soften her views over time, and while I felt she condemned my father unjustly, I sat through her fiery monologues, listening quietly, and was rather relieved when, after a while, she came to adore not only my mother but my father as well.

It did appear that, since independence, the country was intent on self-destruction. Throughout India people were turning on their neighbors, and stories of massacre and murder were never far from anyone's lips. While we were in Simla our treasurer's son was killed as he returned from college in Delhi. His parents couldn't be dissuaded from leaving immediately to try to recover his body, and they were murdered on the train down to Delhi. It was difficult to make sense of any of this destruction of life. Still in Simla, we gave a farewell dinner for Lord Ismay's daughter Sarah and her soon-to-be-fiancé Wenty Beaumont, our ADC. They were on a train to Delhi the next day when a mob of Hindus stopped the train and killed all 150 Muslims on board, with the exception of Wenty's bearer, whom Sarah had bravely hidden beneath her seat, cloaked by her skirt. When the mob burst in, Sarah swore that they were alone in the carriage.

Turmoil was engulfing the newly independent nation, the situation deteriorating with such frightening speed that Congress recalled my father from our brief holiday in Simla. They felt that his advice would be valuable. We traveled back in an open police car, as our car was stuck somewhere between Lucknow and Delhi, leaving Jim Scott, one of the ADCs, with the headache of having to get 80 Muslim and 150 Hindu servants back to Delhi. Eventually it was decided to send them down to Ambala under an armed escort and then fly them home in groups. Our drivers were all Muslim, so we were driven back by the ADCs. In our party was an ecstatic Leela Nand, who was bursting with pride now that he had two "Excellencies" to look after as well as me.

Delhi was a maelstrom. There was a stabbing on the estate soon after we returned and I could not go to the clinic or the canteen without an armed guard, which naturally I did not do as they were needed elsewhere. Anyway, now that a curfew had been imposed, the clinic, which had been looking after two hundred people a day, had very few patients and the canteen was almost empty. The streets were littered with fires and corpses and the ADCs began to find the job of $ADC_2$ the most challenging, as my mother, undeterred by snipers, would get them to help her pick up any corpse she passed in the street and take it to the infirmary. My father had told her that she must have an armed escort but initially she refused, for the same reasons that I had. There was no question of her staying at home, however. She did change her mind after her vehicle was followed by a car full of what she described as "the most terrifying ruffians with guns sticking out everywhere." My father was delighted to know his orders, that armed plainclothes policemen should shadow his wife, had been carried out.

I remained astounded by my mother's stamina and bravery. Before a visit to the Punjab the governor telephoned to say it must be canceled because there was no way he could guarantee her safety, but she insisted on going. The ADC reported that even before landing they could see an enormous crowd below, and when they descended from the plane it was apparent that this was an angry gathering of Sikhs, shouting war cries and brandishing *kirpans*. Assessing the situation, my mother forbade her aides to follow and walked towards the crowd. As she approached, half a dozen of the leaders detached themselves from the mob and moved towards her. The ADCs saw nothing but anger and danger. My mother, however, simply held out her arms towards the leaders, who, to everyone's astonishment, sheathed their weapons and held their arms out too. It was an extraordinary moment, which the ADCs could later only describe to us as one in which love overcame anger. The leaders and my mother hugged and then she moved into the crowd, quickly followed by the ADCs. Her new friends then escorted her to the refugee camp and she was able to do the work she had come to do. There was no question of her being afraid or considering herself brave. She had a job to do and she got on with doing it.

Back in Delhi, the hospitals were woefully vulnerable to attack, and my mother tore around, trying to procure them guards and fuel. Moreover, there was now also the problem of food shortages. Shops were shut, supplies could not get through, and the laborers who produced the food had taken flight. We set up a rationing center on the estate to feed the five thousand residents and the five thousand refugees we had taken in. By the middle of September, it was calculated that the remaining stores of food would last only one more week.

The only good news was that in Calcutta Gandhiji's presence had prevented the terrible rioting that might otherwise have happened there. My father said he alone had accomplished what an army brigade might not have been able to do. When he felt it was time to leave, Gandhiji returned to Delhi, and my father immediately went to talk to him about how best to contain the chaos in the capital. A sort of war room had been set up in the Governor-General's House. Lieutenant General "Pete" Rees came down to head up what became known as the Military Emergency Staff, who were to work out of "the map room." I was drafted in as his PA, typing notes and lists, sending messages, as well as taking and making telephone calls for the general. This would have been quite straightforward had the telephones worked reliably, but they seemed to be forever ringing when you were unable to answer them. And as soon as you were asked to place an urgent call, you would pick up the receiver and find that the line was dead. Most of the telephone operators had left the city. We worked in the map room from nine until six, seven days a week.

When cholera broke out in the refugee camps in Amritsar in the middle of September, my parents flew off with Panditji, Vallabhbhai Patel, Rajkumari Amrit Kaur, and a delegation of representatives to survey the movement of refugees in the Punjab. Jaya went with them as a translator and later told me just how appalled they all were by what they saw, by the sheer numbers of homeless people, and the vast scale of the displacement. Jaya was impressed by my parents' ability to act fairly and speedily and recounted to me how my mother was mobbed wherever she went—it was well known among the refugees that soon after a visit from Lady Mountbatten, help would be close at hand.

The chaos continued throughout October. We were working twelve-hour days, living on bully beef and Spam, under martial law. In the midst of the mayhem, with the country fragmenting around us, it didn't take much to be persuaded by the ADCs that I should join them in seeking a little light relief in a makeshift nightclub set up in the house of an older, rather dashing Indian officer, Brigadier "Kipper" Cariappa. This was my first taste of nightclubbing and I loved it. Kipper had set up a room for dancing, a room for sitting out, and a bar. We were all high on a blitz spirit. Until, that is, Panditji heard about our "club" and had it closed down immediately.

In the midst of all this devastation, I wondered whether we would be able to get away to the wedding of Princess Elizabeth and Philip in November. As a representative of Prince Philip's family, I had been asked to be a bridesmaid— I was lucky that Patricia was already married, otherwise I might have missed out on the privilege. Amid the turbulence of India, the wedding seemed somewhat unreal to me, another world, but I was hoping we would manage to leave the troubles behind us for a short time.

The princess had sent me a sweet letter about the bridesmaids' dresses and the ball the night before the wedding. I had managed to get to the *durzi* in Connaught Circus to have a dress made up from some sari material. I feared we would not be able to leave India, however, as there seemed to be no end to the violence. And indeed, at the end of October, when NWFP tribesmen marched upon Srinagar and Indian troops were sent in to face them, I realized there would be no chance of getting away. My parents agreed that it would be madness for us to leave for England at such a time of trouble. But Panditji thought differently and persuaded them, saying that we should go in order *not* to draw attention to the Kashmir crisis. And so, on 9 November, in spite of our great anxiety, we flew to London for ten days.

## ᴇ 12 ᴇ

The last national celebration, the Victory Parade only a year before, was triumphant but not lighthearted. The royal wedding was to be a moment for the country to rejoice, the first opportunity in years to see so many foreign royals on British soil, after the bleak years of separation that had kept them apart. Unsurprisingly, then, people began to stake out positions along the route in the days before the wedding, and even the promise of rain did nothing to put off the campers intent on glimpsing the heir to the throne on her wedding day.

My seven co-bridesmaids had attended several fittings for their dresses over a period of many weeks. There was only time for me to have two, but the expertise of the designer, Norman Hartnell, and his team meant that the dress fitted perfectly. Our white dresses had an ethereal beauty—tight-waisted with full skirts of many layers of tulle, over white satin petticoats. As they were sleeveless, tulle fichus were draped over our shoulders and fastened with a large satin bow at the front of the bodice. These were edged with a se-ries of star-shaped lily heads created from seed pearls and crystal beads. Our skirts were also sprinkled with the same design, echoing, as we would discover, the pattern covering the bride's tulle train. The fine handiwork in the dresses was set off perfectly by delicate tiaras of silver orange blossom and ears of corn. We wore long white gloves, fastened by a row of half a dozen little pearl buttons so that we could release our hands when it came to eating. I was over the moon to have such a beautiful dress.

During the reception and ball before the wedding, the royal visitors gathered together, the atmosphere one of great excitement as kings and queens, princes and princesses who hadn't seen each other for six years were reunited. So many had been displaced by the war, including high-spirited Queen Frederika of Greece, known as Freddie, who had been exiled to South Africa; Queen Ena, estranged wife of my philandering godfather King Alfonso, who had been in Italy and Switzerland since the 1930s; and King Michael of Romania, who had been crowned king aged five, then exiled to England, and had only just returned to Romania (where a month later he was forced to abdicate at gunpoint by Stalin-backed communists).

I was delighted to see Uncle Gustav and Aunt Louise, my father's sister, and to catch up on family news. I didn't know this at the time but was told later that, during one of the balls, Prince George of Denmark asked Aunt Alice whether she might put a word in for him as my suitor. My father, always one to know his mind, said a firm no, as he believed I was too young and needed to see a bit more of the world before settling down. I was interested to meet the immensely tall King Haakon of Norway. He had refused to collaborate when the Germans occupied his country during the Second World War and he had come to England.

His brother, King Christian X of Denmark, had remained in Copenhagen throughout the war in defiance of the German occupation. He, too, refused to collaborate. Every day he left his palace and rode through the streets on his white horse, showing himself to his people. Crown Princess Juliana of the Netherlands caused a stir, remarking that "Everyone's jewelry is *so* dirty," which may or may not have been the case; to me it was just remarkable that all those royal jewels had survived the war. Most pieces had only just come out of storage for the occasion. It was typical of Princess Juliana to say such a thing, for she was very practical and down-to-earth. When she had been in exile in Canada, her friends and neighbors had noted that she lived happily as one of them without airs or graces. Interestingly, her mother, Queen Wilhelmina, had been an important symbol of Dutch resistance and had brought her government to London. Churchill had described Queen Wilhelmina as the only real man in all the governments-in-exile in London. She was soon to abdicate in favor of her plain-speaking daughter.

The day of the wedding was like being part of a fairy tale. We got ready in Buckingham Palace and the atmosphere was a mixture of frenzy and calm as the professional dressers helped us prepare. As with every wedding there were several moments of panic before the bride was finally ready. As she was having her veil fitted, the tiara broke, so an aide had to be bundled into a taxi and sent across London to the jeweler's. Furthermore, the princess wished to wear the pearls that her father had given her, but after a frantic search, someone remembered that they had been left on display with the other wedding presents at St. James's Palace. Her secretary, Lieutenant Colonel Charteris, was dispatched to retrieve them. Then, just as the bride was about to leave for Westminster Abbey, her bouquet could not be found, and once again there was a lot of rushing around until it was discovered—it had been popped in a cupboard where it would remain cool. Throughout this, the bride remained unflustered and calm.

We traveled by car to Westminster Abbey as the crowd cheered its heart out. At the abbey, those close enough to the barriers were rewarded for their perseverance, as they were the first to see the bride emerge, resplendent in her beautiful dress and veil. Being one of the tallest, I was in the last pair of bridesmaids in the procession, with Princess Margaret and Princess Alexandra at the front to make sure that Princess Elizabeth's veil was in place and the train unfurled before we set off down the aisle. In the rehearsal we had all been warned to veer to the right to avoid walking on the grave of the Unknown Warrior, but one of the little pages, Prince Michael of Kent, stepped right on it.

As we processed slowly up the aisle, I could see Cousin Philip standing with his best man, David Milford Haven, another of our cousins. The bridegroom was so dashing that it made you realize why every girl in England seemed to think she was in love with him. The service was very moving, and as Princess Elizabeth and the newly created Duke of Edinburgh said their vows, the crowd outside could hear every word through the loudspeakers. When the veil was pulled back from Princess Elizabeth's face, everyone could see the beauty of her peaches-and-cream complexion. Once the service was over, a fanfare of trumpets and a rousing organ voluntary accompanied our procession back down the aisle. We followed the newly married couple through the ecstatic crowds back to the palace, closely followed by the king and queen and most of the royalty of Europe.

"Baron," Prince Philip's friend Bill Nahum, had been chosen to take the photographs—much to the chagrin of Cecil

Beaton—and when the bridesmaids were no longer needed, we sat down to watch the huge group being bossed around and the way in which different people responded. Freddie of Greece kept chatting to Juliana of the Netherlands irrespective of instructions; the long bird-of-paradise feathers on my mother's hat obscured several people behind her and Grandmama—no fan of group photographs—positioned herself firmly on the edge of the group, leaving a little space between her and her neighbor, hoping she might be left out of the picture. I thought she looked particularly smart in the long black coat beautifully embroidered in white that my father had brought her from Kashmir. Princess Helena Victoria, known in the family as Thora, was in a wheelchair at the time and held her stick protectively against herself as if she expected the young Prince Richard of Gloucester to do something sudden and unexpected to her. Grandmama, rather mockingly, always referred privately to Thora and her ancient sister Princess Marie Louise as "the Princesses of Nothing," even though they were both granddaughters of Queen Victoria and had been princesses of Schleswig-Holstein. In 1917, when King George V had anglicized everyone's titles, they hadn't gained an English family name.

After the photography session was over, we bridesmaids, the pages, and the best man accompanied the bride and groom, the king and queen, and Queen Mary onto the balcony. We were met by an incredible sight: the police had been holding everyone back around the Victoria Memorial, but when we came out, they let them go and we could see—and hear—a sea of people surging forward. Every time the newlyweds waved, the volume of cheering increased. We were later told that while they were waiting the crowd had been singing "All the Nice Girls Love a Sailor."

We had been on our feet for a long time, so it was a relief to sit down to the wedding breakfast, a splendid banquet of fish and partridge, ice cream and cake for 150 people. After the couple had changed and were ready to leave, we hurried through the palace courtyard to shower them with rose petals. Princess Elizabeth was delighted to discover that Susan, her favorite corgi, had been hidden under a rug in her carriage so that she could join them for their honeymoon at Broadlands; this was particularly poignant for my family as we weren't going to get a chance to go back there before we returned to India. I could only imagine the excitement of the staff as they awaited the royal couple's arrival. Before they left, Philip gave each of the bridesmaids a silver powder compact. Mine had two bands of gold with an *E* and a *P* surmounted by coronets and two bands of gold decoration with six dark-blue sapphires running down the center.

Towards the end of the evening, the bridesmaids went out to dine and dance at a party hosted by David Milford Haven. I hoped—in vain—that Prince Michael of Bourbon-Parma would be there, as he had been by far the most handsome young man at the reception. David was good-looking too but he was older and far more sophisticated than us—his girlfriend at the time was the stunning Swedish model Anita Ekberg—and it was clear he found us dull and prim, for he kept leaping out of his seat and darting over to talk to a dazzling girl at the next table. The girls seated on either side of him looked furious.

The wedding and the attendant celebrations were now over and in no time at all we had to leave England. "Lovely to be home," my father wrote in his diary once we were back in India. We were still laughing at Queen Mary's reaction to the piece of specially woven white cotton that we had brought from Gandhiji for Princess Elizabeth and Philip. When the gift was displayed, Queen Mary was horrified to discover what she took to be "a loincloth." For us, there was now a sense of familiarity to life in Delhi, and a sense of belonging. And so it was that we vowed to make the most of our remaining, precious time in India.

My parents dressed for the coronation of King George VI, 1937

With Pandit Nehru, 1948

Broadlands with Neola, 1948

With the former viceroy and Lady Wavell on arrival in India

Saying farewell on the steps of Viceroy's House with Pandit Nehru and Chakravarti Raja-gopalachari, who succeeded my father as governor general

Photograph by Cecil Beaton, 1948

Princess
Elizabeth
presenting
a cup to my
father in
Malta, 1949

Winning the Ladies Race in Malta, 1949

Fijian chief making a presentation to the queen, 1953

My mother and I enjoying a Japanese teahouse in Delhi in 1959 with Pandit Nehru and his daughter, Indira Gandhi

Portrait by Terence Donovan, 1959. The beginning of my new life

## ❧ 13 ❧

On our return it was clear that the postpartition crisis was far from over. Now that he was governor-general—a merely decorative title—my father decided to reinforce the message of independence by leaving the new government to its business and honoring the tradition of visiting the princely states. It was to be an arduous undertaking by my parents and the ADCs. My father was a stickler for precision and such a tour was demanding on his staff—they had to ensure protocol was observed, all schedules ran to time, and no one was offended. This was no easy task.

Our party now always contained extra guests because my parents, thinking that we would have plenty of time to entertain them, had extended invitations to their friends. Sadly, this proved not to be the case, and the friends were often dragged along in our retinue or left pretty much to their own devices until we returned. As I was reminded each morning on our ride, my father was delighted that Yola was to be our first visitor, accompanied by another friend, Kay Norton. She had once found her bearer looking through a keyhole into her room. When reprimanded he replied, quite obviously, "But if I don't, how do I know when to go in?"

They would accompany us to the much-anticipated silver

jubilee celebrations of His Highness the Maharaja of Jaipur. This weeklong celebration promised to be a magnificent affair, but we were worried by the continuing riots in the Punjab. The European guests invited to the jubilee were woefully ignorant of the situation in the north and my father was extremely irritated by the glamorous Princess Peggy d'Arenberg and her friend Rosita de Rosière, who arrived from Paris with a personal hairdresser. He thought this very bad form when there were starving and displaced Indians all around.

My parents were already friends with the Jaipur family. The maharaja was an international polo player and had often played in England, and they kept a house in London. I had got to know them in Delhi as his son Bubbles was the commandant of the bodyguard. I was surprised that Ayesha, although Jai's constant companion in Delhi as "third her highness in Jaipur," was very much the junior hostess to "second her highness," Jo Didi. I was also surprised to discover that although Jai was only in his midthirties, he had three wives (one of whom had died a couple of years earlier), five children (two of whom were older than me), and had been ruler of his state for a quarter of a century.

This was the first time I had visited Jai's palaces. He lived in the private apartments of the huge City Palace, some of which had already been turned into a museum. There seemed to be palaces all over the place—we stayed in the enormous Rambagh Palace, and on a ride on the back of an elephant to the Amber Fort, we saw three more palaces hidden in the steep defile below.

The festivities began with a grand parade for the festival of Dussehra, when Hindus mark the triumph of good over evil. We watched men in turbans and courtly dress carrying huge ceremonial horns and magnificently bedecked elephants process slowly past us in the palace courtyard. It was a shock to see Jai sacrifice a goat, dip his fingers into little bowls of its blood, then, with a flicking movement, bless a long line of elaborately dressed horses, oxen, and elephants as each was brought to him. When the celebrations moved to the palace hall, my parents were placed in positions of honor just to the left of Jai, who sat on a great throne made of pure silver. There he received a long procession of nobles who had arrived to pay homage, kept cool as they waited by the ministrations of servants with huge plumed fans. It was a world away from the civil war that was rapidly becoming imminent five hundred miles to the north in Kashmir.

A couple of days into the celebrations my father invested Jai as grand commander of the Star of India in the City Palace, and I found myself seated next to the old Maharaja of Kapurthala. It was a relief to be able to talk to him—when I had first met him, soon after our arrival, it had been very awkward as he kept asking me if I had been able to do any sightseeing. I had only been to the Qutub Minar tower with my mother, but I didn't like to mention it because his young, sixth wife had just committed suicide by jumping from it. This time I was not so tongue-tied.

We returned to Delhi after six wonderful days—my father in cheerful mood as Jai had organized for him to play in a polo match at which he was reunited with Rao Raja Hanut Singh, the very man who had taught him to play in Jodhpur in 1921. I was particularly excited about returning as Patricia and John were coming to stay. Sadly they didn't bring their baby as it would have been too unsettling for him. Apparently they noticed a great difference in me, and remarked on how serious I had become since swapping my life as an English schoolgirl for that of the last viceroy of India's daughter. I came in for a lot of teasing and was nicknamed "Lady Earnestine."

At the final gathering of the Chamber of Princes, my father tried his best to see that the princes were left as secure as possible within the new dominions. He felt strongly that they needed to understand they were responsible for their own destiny. With this in mind he advised them to take up any opportunity that presented itself, and many did find their feet in the new political landscape: Jai became ambassador to Spain, Patiala became the chief minister in Patiala State, and the new Maharaja of Kashmir, Tiger, enjoyed a brilliant career in India. And while some never recovered from the shock of their changed circumstances, others found themselves on unexpected journeys. Several years later, my father was very surprised to see the young Rao Raja of Bundi—a seventeen-gun-salute prince and Second World War hero, awarded an MC in Burma—standing behind the president of India's chair at a banquet as the president's ADC. My father's ADCs had always sat down to eat with us. Bundi asked to see him afterwards and my father feared he was going to complain. He was very surprised when Bundi merely wanted to express his gratitude to my father for having encouraged him to offer the president his services.

Meanwhile, as violence continued to sweep through the country, Gandhiji was about to fast again "unto death," or until the Muslim and Hindu leaders promised to make peace. The numbers of dead were rising and millions of people had been forced to flee their homes. The situation was the very antithesis of what Gandhiji stood for, and he felt India had learned nothing from all the years he had spent teaching nonviolence and brotherhood. His silent protests had been very effective in the past, and this time he was showing his distress that Congress was withholding partition payments from Pakistan by way of sanction, again vowing to continue his fast until it relented.

It was decided we would all still travel to Bikaner as part of my father's tour, but that as a mark of respect for the fast there would be no state banquet. A party of twenty-eight, we stayed with the maharaja, and were presented with a sixty-page program for the days ahead. The entry for Lagoon Terrace read, "The Master of the Household will take the necessary steps to ensure that the crows and other birds are not allowed to settle on trees on the Lagoon Terrace for at least a week beforehand and special care must be taken about this on the day of the lunch." It was, though, a particularly enjoyable visit as my father had known the maharaja for many years. They had first met when they were children, later at the coronation of King George V, and then when my father served on the staff of the Prince of Wales for his visit to India in 1921.

There was an early-morning shoot of the famous imperial sandgrouse. Thirty thousand birds flew over our heads. They were difficult to shoot, flying very fast and swerving in all directions. That evening we gathered in the Durbar Hall of Lallgarh Palace where my father invested the maharaja with the Grand Cross of the Star of India. The assembled nobles and courtiers looked magnificent in their red and yellow Durbar dress.

The next day, a review of the Bikaner State Army included a trot past of the Camel Corps and a gallop past of the Durbar Lancers. The Bijey Battery on parade served with great distinction in my father's Burma campaign in the Second World War and also fought in the battles of Kohima and Imphal.

We then visited the fort where we saw regalia given to the Bikaner rulers by Mughal emperors and were shown beautifully illuminated Sanskrit and Urdu manuscripts.

Immediately we arrived back in Dehli, my parents went to see Gandhi at Birla House and found him very weak but not without his desire to tease. "It takes a fast to bring you to me," he reproached them with a smile. Five days after he began his fast, Congress relented and paid over the money to Pakistan. Gandhiji had remained characteristically composed both during his fast and after a bomb exploded in his garden two days later.

There are no words to express the shock, that moment of horror, when two weeks later, as I was listening to the wireless in my room, having returned from a visit with my parents to the Central States, it was announced that Gandhiji had been assassinated. At first I could not believe what I was hearing but the gravity of the announcer's voice was unmistakable, and as the tears poured down my cheeks I felt as if I had lost a member of my family. It would not be an exaggeration to say that the whole of India came to a complete standstill, everyone stunned by the death of the Father of the Nation.

In the chaotic hours that followed, it was not clear who had been the assassin. When my father arrived at Birla House, someone in the crowd shouted, "A Muslim did it!" My father had to think quickly, for such an unfounded rumor could incite civil war. "You fool!" he shouted back. "It was a Hindu!" He was proved right, the assassin a Hindu fanatic from the RSS Party. Inside the building my father found the country's leaders in silent reverence, lost in their distress at the death of their mentor and friend. Nehru had somehow to pull himself together to make a broadcast to the nation that afternoon. The simplicity of his words, "The light has gone out," summed up our collective feelings perfectly.

In keeping with the Hindu custom to cremate a body as soon as possible after death, Gandhiji's funeral was arranged for the next day. His body had been laid on the balcony at Birla House and in death he seemed so tiny and frail, his head resting peacefully on a cushion of flowers. At first I couldn't work out why he didn't look like himself, then I realized that his glasses had been removed. His body was carried down to the funeral carriage and covered with the new Indian national flag. Everywhere the crowds pressed in, trying to touch him, and it was a while before the procession was able to start. The Mahatma's last journey, accompanied by large crowds of his fellow countrymen, was to take him to the Raj Ghat, the burning ground six miles away on the banks of the holy River Jumna. At the head of the procession, next to the bier, Nehru led the people, a slow, solemn journey on foot.

We went ahead by car, followed by the Indian governors. At the Raj Ghat we pushed our way through the enormous gathering to a low platform in front of the funeral pyre. In the distance we could see the slow approach of the cortège, followed by hundreds of thousands of mourners. My father, realizing that the sheer pressure of such an emotional crowd might push all those in the front ranks onto the pyre, rushed up and down instructing the ambassadors, governors, and assorted VIPs to sit cross-legged on the ground. In a highly charged atmosphere, Gandhiji's body was placed on the funeral pyre. After it was anointed with sacred oils and showered with ghee, Gandhiji's son lit the pyre. It was horrific to see his beloved body engulfed by flames, but strangely the atmosphere of intense sorrow soon changed to one of joy as people in the crowd pressed forward to throw flowers.

Momentarily, the new feeling of elation changed to shock as several village women screamed hysterically and tried to hurl themselves into the flames to commit suttee, but mercifully they were stopped before they could harm themselves. As the fire consumed Gandhiji's body, the air became filled with cries of "Gandhi is immortal!"

Gandhiji's ashes were to be scattered in Allahabad at the confluence of the two sacred rivers, the Ganges and the Jumna. So it was decided that the forthcoming Mela—when hundreds of thousands of people come together to bathe in holy waters on the first day of the new moon—would be an auspicious time to take them. Allahabad, by coincidence, was also the place of Panditji's birth and so, a little over a week after the assassination, we set off with Panditji to make the journey. We did so with mixed feelings of sorrow at the heaviness of the duty that was to be performed and excitement at the prospect of seeing the Mela with the man who was rapidly becoming a close and very special friend.

When we arrived at Allahabad there was a memorial service at the Cathedral Church of the Redemption for Gandhiji, where we sang his favorite hymns, including "Abide with Me," and my father read a lesson. Gandhiji's ashes were scattered in the water, where hundreds of pilgrims had gathered—fully clothed women, near-naked sadhus adorned in white body paint, some standing up to their knees, others to their waists, others submerged completely in the holy waters.

Although it was a deeply sorrowful time, it was a comfort to spend more time with Panditji and get used to his ways. He was apt to fall into long periods of silence and reflection, but he was never aloof with us. When he was not his normal animated self you realized that he was wrestling with some incredibly important problem and needed to be left alone, but soon he would be full of charm again. His moods could change very quickly and he was often quick to anger, such as on the day when too many people gave my parents autograph books to sign and the crowd became overwhelming. Suddenly Panditji's mood changed and he seized all the books and threw them into the air. My mother was very taken aback but his smile returned just as quickly and he put his arm around our shoulders and we laughed and everything felt fine again.

There was no sign at this time that my mother's regard for Nehru was anything other than deep friendship, but during a short break at the Retreat in the Himalayas to help him recover his energy, a profound connection developed between them. Now, just six weeks before we were due to leave India, she found in Panditji the companionship and equality of spirit and intellect that she craved. Each helped overcome loneliness in the other. Nehru had been a widower for ten years and had also recently lost the company of his family: his daughter, Mrs. Gandhi, was rarely around as she was married with young children and was much involved in the Congress Party; one sister, Nan Pandit, was now ambassador to Moscow and the other, Betty Hutheesing, lived in Bombay.

As we left the heat of the plains and traveled up into the hills, journeying to the Retreat at Mashobra, in the wooded hillside above Simla, my mother was easy to get along with, and a sense of well-being emanated from her. My father and I were very tactful, falling behind her and Nehru as we walked together or leaving the room when they were deep in conversation. But we did not, at any time, feel excluded. Our small party did everything together, most memorably taking a long drive into the mountains to see Tibet at a distance. At night we all played racing demons or parlor games (not my father's favorite pastime) or simply sat reading peacefully together.

My parents' modus vivendi would hold fast but it was particularly easy in this instance, for my father trusted them both. His life was made easier too now that my mother's newfound happiness released him from the relentless late-night recriminations. In recent months, whenever he had left his huge pile of paperwork to go up to say good night to her, my father would find himself subject to a long string of accusations that he didn't understand: he was ignoring her, his behavior had been rude, and he didn't care about her. He was sympathetic and apologized, even though he did not understand what he had done wrong. These were the exhausted outpourings of a woman who always drove herself too hard and felt intellectually isolated. To my father's great relief, after our short stay in the mountains, these sessions ceased. Now when my father went up he would find her studying her pocket atlas, and she would simply smile and wish him a cheery "Good night, Dickie, darling." He would then return to work through most of the night without a heavy heart.

In later years, reading Panditji's inner thoughts and feelings in his letters to my mother, I came to realize how deeply he and my mother loved and respected each other. I had been curious as to whether or not their affair had been sexual in nature; having read the letters, I was utterly convinced it hadn't been. Quite apart from the fact that neither my mother nor Panditji had time to indulge in a physical affair, they were rarely alone. They were always surrounded by staff, police, and other people, and as my father's ADC, Freddie Burnaby Atkins, told me later, it would have been impossible for them to have been having an affair, such was the very public nature of their lives.

Our final few weeks in India whirled by, my mother still making tours of the refugee camps. In Kurukshetra and Panipat, the refugees had crowded around in their thousands to say good-bye. Even more moving was the fact that refugees from other camps had clubbed together to buy a railway ticket so that each camp could send a representative with a small gift as a token of their gratitude.

A few days before we were to leave, a book arrived for me from Panditji. "I am sending you a little book about myself!" he wrote. "It is meant for children. I have to add that my sending you this book does not mean to imply that I do not respect your mature wisdom." He always managed to make me laugh. My mother wanted to give Panditji a gift—her precious emerald ring—but she knew he would not accept it. Instead, she handed it to his daughter, Indira, telling her that if he were ever to find himself in financial difficulties—he was well known for giving away all his money—she should sell it for him.

Our last day was overwhelming. We began with a drive through Old Delhi, waving to crowds estimated to be over a quarter of a million strong, and then we returned to Governor-General's House for a farewell party for all two thousand staff. In the evening we attended our last state banquet in the house, hosted by the cabinet. It was a bittersweet occasion. Panditji made moving speeches about both my parents, praising my father and thanking him profoundly. I was overcome with shyness as he thanked me for "coming straight from school and possessing all the charm she does," for doing "a grown-up person's work in the troubled scene of India." Most poignantly he addressed my mother directly, saying, "Wherever you have gone, you have brought solace, you have brought hope and encouragement. Is it surprising therefore that the people of India should love you and look up to you as one of themselves and should grieve that you are going?"

As we prepared to leave I found myself overcome with sorrow as I said good-bye to Leela Nand. He was still recovering from the tragic death of his seven-year-old son three months earlier, and while I had done all I could to comfort him, I knew he was broken inside. We clung to each other, tears rolling down our cheeks. As we left Governor-General's House for the last time we descended the long flight of steps lined by the bodyguard and got into the carriage with the mounted escort drawn up behind. Suddenly one of the horses jibbed and a voice shouted out, "Even the horses won't let you go." This cry was taken up and repeated by the crowd. My mother and I waved through our tears, trying to keep on smiling.

At Palam airport the incoming governor-general, Chakravarti Rajagopalachari, our dear friend Rajaji, wept as he embraced my mother in farewell. Nevertheless she managed to smile as she shook hands with row upon row of officials before we climbed into the plane. As we took our places, I saw her fumbling with something around her neck, an urgency to her movements that betrayed her calm exterior. She whispered something to her PA and passed her something in a closed fist, motioning for her to leave the plane. It was only later that I discovered the PA had been sent out with my mother's precious St. Christopher to find a safe pair of hands to get it to Panditji. The long flight home passed in somber silence.

Landing at Northolt, we were greeted by a host of people including Prince Philip, Clement Attlee, the prime minister, Krishna Menon, and Patricia. After the formal greetings my father made a short statement to the press and then my mother, now dressed immaculately for the British summer in a suit, hat, and fur stole, stepped onto the dais to make a speech. She could only just control her emotions. She spoke first of the people of India, who she said had "shown us such unbelievable confidence and generosity and affection." Then she added, "I shall always think back on our time in India with"—and here she began to falter, and had difficulty in getting the words out—"every . . . possible . . . feeling." She stopped, blinked, then licked her lower lip until for a horrifying moment I thought she might break down. Then, as she turned to my father for support, he gave her a warm, confident smile and she regained her composure and found the strength to continue, ". . . with happiness, as well as sorrow, for what the people have been through. But I am grateful to India and I will always regard India as a second home." And with that the photographers' bulbs popped, we shook more hands, and drove off to our other home.

## ~~~ 14 ~~~

I missed India. I missed Leela Nand, I missed Panditji, I missed the noise and chaos of the clinic, and I even missed the long marble corridors of Governor-General's House. I was finding it difficult to adapt to life back at Broadlands, roaming around the house moodily or standing in the schoolroom twiddling the knobs on the wireless in search of the faint crackle of Indian music. It was some compensation that we had brought Neola with us—he didn't seem to mind which continent he made mischief in, and spent his days turning my bedroom into a mongoose stronghold. Downstairs there was a little more to remind me of India as my parents had brought their bearers, Wahid Beg and Abdul Hamid, to Broadlands. Both were Muslim and it was thought they might fare better away from Delhi when we left. To me they seemed rather lost in England, shivering in the navy-blue waistcoats they had worn in Simla. Seeing them in their uniform brought on a wave of nostalgia, but these small touches of India did not make me feel that I belonged back in England.

I wrote to Panditji, initially to thank him for all the kind presents he had given me before we left, but the letter became a reflection on all that I had experienced in India. My letter crossed in the post with the first of his, dated five days after our departure. He was missing us too: "A visit to Kashmir always cheers me up and so today I felt a little better than I have done since the Mountbattens left." He added that "not being a slave to duty like your mother"—not *exactly* true, I reflected—he had felt sufficiently low to take some rare time out to walk in the mountains, swim, and do some "surf riding." He described a wrestling match which although he had lost he had enjoyed "thoroughly and immediately after spoke at a meeting for an hour and a quarter." His opponent "had not fared so well and had to apply various balms and ointments! I am rather sorry for him but I must confess that I have gone up in my own estimation. Obviously it must be due to my standing on my head. I am sorry you have not taken to this." I was even happier with his next letter that responded to my one in which I had recorded my thoughts about my time in his country. It had revealed to him, he wrote, that not only was I a good letter writer but someone with "inner depths who is on a voyage of discovery." I was flattered and even more moved by the advice that followed as it crystallized perfectly so many of the emotions I had been experiencing since our return to England.

"It is a fascinating business not only to grow in every way but to be conscious of that growth," he wrote. "I entirely agree with you that it was more worthwhile for you to witness and feel the extraordinary things happening in India during the past year and more than to lead just a comfortable unexciting life. Unhappily we have to pay in life for everything worthwhile. If we want experience, depth and an understanding of life's infinite phases we have to suffer shock and sorrow and then, if we are strong enough to rise above them, life is a curious bittersweet affair. Too much of its bitter aspect is of course terrible, but too much of unalloyed sweetness can also be bad enough. So your experiences in India may perhaps have fitted you a little for your future journeys through life and given you a broader and deeper vision. How I envy your youth with the adventure of life stretching out before you." He signed off "with my love and yours affectionately, Mamu Jawaharlal." Seeing the affectionate signing off as Mamu brought back fond memories of his wish for me to call him Uncle, something that my father at the time had thought a little too familiar.

I also wrote to Leela Nand. Ever since the death of his son I had always been concerned for him. When the reply came it was written by his brother Amla, who expressed his sorrow that Leela could not reply in person. Leela Nand, who was just thirty-six and perfectly healthy, had died. He had not shot himself, he had not taken poison or thrown himself out of a window. Leela Nand had merely lain down and died because he willed it. He died of a broken heart. I stood with the letter in my hand, trying to take in the shock of this dreadful news.

Grandmama was relieved that she had lived long enough to see us all safely back home. I had missed her hugely and in turn was relieved to see that in spite of the ever-present chilblains on her poor fingers and toes, she was surprisingly well. On a trip to the British Museum, I went to pick her up from Kensington Palace, intending to hail a taxi to take us to Bloomsbury. "A taxi, dear child?" she asked, setting off, best foot forward, towards the nearest bus stop. As the bus pulled away, she ran ahead, while I followed breathlessly, just managing to jump on behind her. Sensitive to my ennui, she picked up on the difficulties I was having in reacclimatizing. She remarked drily, "We have many beautiful things in this country too, my dear. When you go to stay with Patricia, ask her to take you to Canterbury Cathedral."

And slowly, I did begin to enjoy myself again in England. To my delight, my family was invited to attend the opening ceremony of the 1948 Olympic Games in London, and from the royal box we were swept up in the pride of each team as they came past the royal family. We were rather shocked as the American team fell out of step and began taking photographs of the king and queen. We even took the Shah of Iran—at the time a charming, progressive, and enthusiastic young man—to see the show *Oklahoma!* and then on to dinner and dancing at the Savoy. It was the first time I had driven with a police escort in London and certainly the first time that the car in which I was being driven had ignored any red traffic lights. The day after that, I was on my way to stay with Patricia when I met the shah's chamberlain on the station platform, waiting for the same train. The chamberlain was very gallant, and as the train pulled up, he threw open the door of a first-class compartment for me. I, however, was on a very strict allowance and had a third-class ticket. Being a courteous man, he got in with me. I could see from his expression that he had never traveled third-class before but manners prevailed over comfort and that was fortunate for me as he made a delightful companion down to Kent.

It also helped to be surrounded by so many guests that summer, and we enjoyed a particular rowdy weekend with Yola, Prince Philip, his sister Tiny, and her husband, Prince George of Hanover. After dinner one evening Philip did his wonderful imitation of a coy lady preparing for a bath, complete with imaginary slipping towel, and our mood was so buoyant we finished the evening with some rather mad games. It was all too much for Yola, who left the next morning. *"Non, non!"* she cried. *"C'est trop fatigant!"* She never could cope with more than one or two of us at a time, let alone an overexcited gaggle.

Neola spent most of his time upstairs, settled on a hot pipe—though once in a deep sleep his little paws would relax and he would fall off—or creating havoc in the schoolroom. During tea one afternoon, my father asked me to bring Neola downstairs so that we could show him to our guests. These were no ordinary guests, for that particular weekend they included the king, queen, Princess Margaret, and two of her friends, Johnny Dalkeith and David Ogilvy. "Nonsense, darling," my father said as I tried to make excuses, "I am sure everyone would love to see him. Elizabeth, you would love to, wouldn't you?" And the queen, ever polite and charming, said, "Yes, of course we would love to, Dickie." So, with a great deal of apprehension, I collected Neola, returning with him on my shoulder as the guests clustered round. The king—who suffered from lumbago and was renowned for his short temper—heaved himself out of his armchair and made polite noises about my mongoose. Then, with an audible sigh of relief, he went back to his chair and slowly lowered himself into it. At this precise moment, Neola took fright, jumped from my shoulder, and leapt onto the back of the king's chair so that monarch and mongoose collided. The king leapt up and Johnny called out wittily, "Ah, a sovereign cure for lumbago!" We all laughed until we noticed that the king was not so amused. We held our breath waiting for an explosion, but then he sighed wearily and sat back down.

Before he agreed to take the position of viceroy, my father had made it a condition that on his return he could resume his career in the navy. He had now been appointed to command the First Cruiser Squadron in the Mediterranean Fleet, returning to the service with his real rank, that of rear admiral, well below the substantive position he had held as supreme allied commander and the giddy heights of viceroyalty. In the pecking order of seniority, he would rank thirteenth, something he thought would help keep his ego in check. But this caused huge confusion for the commander in chief—whom my father now addressed as "sir" as he had served under my father in SEAC and kept slipping back into old habits, absentmindedly addressing *him* as "sir." Poor Sir Arthur John Power also had to deal with Prince Philip, who, joining the fleet as a junior officer, called him "sir." Mindful that Prince Philip was married to the heir to the throne, the C in C couldn't help but address his junior officer as "sir."

When we left that summer to spend some time with Yola and Henri, my mother warned me to pack a black dress, "just in case," as Henri was now very old—forty years older than Yola—and his health was often poor. In fact, the indefatigable Henri was in fine spirits and welcomed us with open arms. "*Bon!* You are here finally. *Dépêchez-vous*, I have tickets for the Folies Bergère tonight!" He also used his influence to get me into the casino, as I was still under age, but being the Lady Earnestine that I was, I was most disapproving of the goings-on inside. It was lovely to be back in Monte Carlo for an evening, however, as I had fond memories of the last time I had been there, my sister, mother, and I creating Princess Plink and Plonk costumes for Bunny's photo from the hotel room furnishings. Before we left France, my father, ever the enthusiast, insisted on buying underwater goggles, harpoon guns, and snorkels. He had been talking to Jacques Cousteau and his interest in underwater fishing began to take hold.

Back at Broadlands, we started to pack for Malta,

although we continued to welcome guests to the house. I was delighted to see Krishna Menon, still the high commissioner for India in the UK, who was full of news about the surrender of Hyderabad to Indian government troops and, significantly, the death of Mr. Jinnah. No one else, apart from his doctors and sister, had known how ill he was all through the partition talks, and I reflected on how it must have hardened his determination to create Pakistan at all costs. A week before we left, Nehru came to England for the Commonwealth Prime Ministers' Conference, and he managed to find time to visit us at Broadlands. He was extremely playful with Patricia's children, getting down on all fours in the drawing room and making lion faces at Norton and his new brother, Michael John, who roared back in absolute delight.

Neola settled into life in Malta in his own inimitable way. We stayed at the newly opened Hotel Phoenicia while waiting for the refurbishment of our rented house to be complete, and Neola had to stay with us. Returning one afternoon, we found the lobby of the hotel in uproar, two maids gesticulating wildly at the manager. As soon as I heard the words "A rat! It was a rat!" I knew that Neola had to be involved, and as the maids pointed in my direction, my fears were confirmed. Neola had escaped while we were out, run down to the floor below, and found his way into another room. The occupant, a recovering alcoholic as it happened, was suffering from delirium tremens accompanied by frequent sightings of "pink elephants." He had been advised by his doctor that when he suffered such a delusion, he should "sit on it" to prove there was nothing there, so when he had returned to his room to find a strange creature on his chair, he'd simply walked over and sat on it. A mongoose bites hard—and hangs on—and the poor man's screams could be heard throughout the hotel.

It was a relief to the hotel authorities when we moved out. In our small garden at Villa Guardamangia, Neola scampered down the paths that ran between dusty flower beds, in and out of the bright geraniums, marigolds, and snapdragons, and ferreted about in the bougainvillea that grew up the apricot-colored walls of the house. He basked in the sun, as did my mother whenever she had the chance. My parents had always been very happy in Malta, and being back seemed to give my father a renewed love of life—and speed, as he hurtled around the island in his eye-catching black and pale-blue Riley with its silver sailor mascot, or dashed out to sea on the admiral's barge. He also began to indulge his new passion for spearfishing, acquiring compressed-air tanks and resurfacing only when he had caught his prized *dorade*. Conscious that it would be highly irresponsible to endanger himself while underwater, he was always careful to decompress properly when coming to the surface. When asked whether he preferred polo or scuba diving, he thought for a moment before replying, "Well, polo is *only* a game."

During the day, I became a caseworker for the Soldiers, Sailors, Airmen Families Association (SSAFA) and joined the office that concentrated on the domestic welfare of those men serving overseas. We had an office in the army headquarters in the Castille, one of the beautiful buildings of the Knights of St. John in Valletta. Nearly all my time was spent with old Mrs. Bonnici, whose son was serving in the RAF and kept bombarding his commanding officer with anxious inquiries about his eighty-year-old mother. She lived in a village at the other end of the island, and I would drive out to see her before making my report. She was always well, regaling me with coffee and sticky cakes as we conversed in gestures and giggles. There was never anything untoward to report and yet Airman Bonnici's commanding officer demanded that I go again and again.

My mother was working with the St. John Ambulance Brigade and the Save the Children Fund on top of her duties as the wife of the admiral commanding a cruiser squadron. She kept up an almost daily correspondence with Panditji, but although she also had time to relax she was finding Malta parochial after her enormous responsibilities as vicereine. At the end of 1949, she asked me to come with her to India on her visit to inspect the Refugee Relief and Rehabilitation Committee she had set up after partition. It was wonderful to see Panditji again and the three of us visited museums and galleries. He was so knowledgeable about his country's past, and on that trip he brought Indian history and art alive for us. His friendship had opened my mother's eyes to the beauty of art, and his encouragement continued even when they were apart, for his letters to her often included snatches of poetry or long quotations from books he had read or vivid descriptions of things he had seen. My mother seemed to flourish in his company, so happy and fulfilled in his presence.

Soon after we returned to Malta, and much to the delight of the island, Princess Elizabeth came to welcome Prince Philip back with the fleet. I went with her to watch the magnificent sight of fifty ships coming into port, in immaculate formation, firing a twenty-one-gun salute in front of the Fort of St. Elmo as the princess flew her standard. The prince and princess then came to stay with us at Villa Guardamangia, the island so small that it was almost possible for Princess Elizabeth to live the life of a normal naval officer's wife. We often ate at home or went out for dinner and dancing at the Marsa, and they joined us on several family expeditions in the admiral's barge. One evening, the princess proudly showed us the films she had taken herself of her son Charles, who was now walking and was very sweet. And sometimes, when they wanted just to be alone, Prince Philip and his wife went out together, driving in the little Hillman, their plain-clothes police officer a discreet distance behind.

I officially came of age in Malta, turning twenty-one on 19 April. I was awoken by a strange cacophony and on closer, sleepy inspection found a group singing "Happy Birthday to You" and "Twenty-one Today," to the accompaniment of the C in C's bandsmen, who were clearly bewildered at being made to play silly tunes at the top of Guardamangia Hill at 8 a.m. I celebrated two days later with the princess on her twenty-fourth birthday, at the Phoenicia, complete with Scottish reels and country dances. "The Dashing White Sergeant" traditionally broke the ice at the beginning of the evening and the reels allowed the other officers to pluck up the courage to ask the heir to the throne to dance. She danced extremely well and loved it. These were happy, carefree days for the princess. When the time came for her to return to England, my mother remarked that it was like putting a little bird back in its gilded cage.

In May, my father's term commanding the First Cruiser Squadron was over and we returned to Broadlands. My mother set about, with typical Mountbatten vigor, restoring the now-vacated rooms—the hospital had moved out the year before—to their former glory. I needed something to immerse myself in and, with Krishna Menon's encouragement, intended to apply to the office of the Indian High Commission. When the moment came, however, my father took me to one side and suggested that it would be best, diplomatically, to put a little distance between our family and India. Churchill was still not speaking to my father for the part he had played in what Churchill called "giving away the jewel in her crown." This was a disappointment to me, for while I enjoyed my work at SSAFA—and was happy to continue—I had hoped to have official ties to India once more. The beautiful bookends that Panditji sent from Srinagar for my birthday went a little way towards cheering me up, and I settled back into my work.

My parents felt that as I had an allowance I should not take paid work when somebody else probably needed the job far more than I did. And I felt that taking pay from SSAFA, a charity, would not have been right. Much to my frustration, I was told that I could not work in the onward transmission office because only paid employees not voluntary workers staffed it. Yet this was where I felt I could be of most use following my experience in Malta, compiling the reports on which the COs depended when considering whether to grant compassionate leave to men serving overseas. I decided to appeal to the office chief, Colonel Batten, but he seemed immovable, keen only to get rid of me as his office had a mountain of work to get through. I asked whether he needed more help, and for a moment he seemed to forget why I was there, and confided that his funds didn't make that possible. Seizing my chance, I suggested he take me on as he wouldn't have to pay me and I would need only a typewriter, a small table, and a chair. He tutted, frowned, and, mustache bristling, muttered, "Most irregular." But then he agreed to a week's trial, so I was in. And I stayed.

Once again, Grandmama was delighted to see us on our return from a spell abroad. She was now eighty-seven and I noticed that she was beginning to slow down. She stayed with us at Broadlands all summer, but was not always the easiest person to manage, as she certainly was not of the opinion that she had slowed down at all. One afternoon, I packed a tea basket and we set off across the long sweep of lawn that bordered the orangery. When we turned a corner and the house vanished from sight, I steered us towards a gravel path that led to a bench from which there was a beautiful view over the river. Grandmama had not stopped talking for a moment, constantly stopping and turning sideways to address me, which normally would have been maddening but on this occasion was a relief. Eventually we reached the bench and she suddenly went quiet as she realized that we were only fifty yards from the house. She was so angry that she refused to have tea and insisted we return to the house at once, ignoring the pain of her chilblained toes. She was dreadfully insulted and kept up a silent protest long into the evening.

Sadly, as the summer wore on, my grandmother declined further. Her mind was as active as ever but the appalling circulation she had suffered all her life got worse, as did the chilblains. Playing her beloved patience became torture and life ceased to be a pleasure. When she returned to Kensington Palace she contracted severe bronchitis and fell gravely ill. Death did not come immediately, and on several occasions she went to sleep expecting to die in the night, then was most annoyed with herself when she awoke again in the morning. Far be it from Grandmama to waste the extra time; she used it to remind Isa that as she was going to be buried in Whippingham on the Isle of Wight, it would be very cold crossing the Solent, so Isa should be sure to wear her warm boots.

When Grandmama died, even though we all felt that she had been ready to go, we suffered her loss most acutely. She had been a constant source of support and comfort to me, providing me with much-needed stability during my childhood. Her lively mind, sharp wit, and fascinating stories had kept me entertained throughout my life, and her manners, bearing, and relentless lack of self-pity had been an inspiration. We held a family service in the Chapel Royal, then accompanied her coffin from London to Portsmouth and on, by naval frigate, to the Isle of Wight, where we laid her to rest beside her beloved husband.

## ~~~ 15 ~~~

My grandfather had been with King George V on his visit to India and my father had accompanied the Prince of Wales, later King Edward VIII, on his tour to India, Australia, and Japan. My father was therefore keen for me to continue the family tradition, and as such I was invited to go on the Commonwealth Tour with Princess Elizabeth as one of her two ladies-in-waiting. I wasn't happy about this. Having settled back into life in England after India and Malta, I just wanted to stay at home. But I had no choice, really, and at a reception at Buckingham Palace, Queen Mary rather alarmingly confirmed that I was going on the tour, telling me, "You must remember that you will be 'in waiting' and so you are to call her 'Princess Elizabeth' and 'ma'am' and *never* Lilibet." It seemed my fate was sealed.

The princess confided that she wanted me to go with her as Philip might have a different program from her at times and we could have a good giggle together. The palace gave me a dress allowance, so I was able to go to my mother's couturier, Worth, for half a dozen or so expensive items. It was a heady experience, though the fittings for each dress and coat somewhat dampened the fun. I was thrilled with the result for I would need to be suitably dressed for a broad range

of occasions—balls, receptions, cocktail parties, garden parties—and would need silk dresses for day wear and a couple
of cotton dresses in case I got the day off, not to mention the
coats, hats, shoes, handbags, and gloves that were de rigueur.
After the lengthy dress fittings and nasty immunization jabs
at the Hospital for Tropical Diseases, Henriette Palmer, the
lady-in-waiting who was accompanying me, came round to
brief me. She told me to try to persuade people not to give
the princess puce-colored flowers and above all to "mind
the bookie." As I knew nothing about racing this was most
alarming. I must have looked blank as she went on to explain
that if the princess was given more than one—*bouquet*, not
bookie, I realized with relief—which was usually the case,
she would hand the previous one over to the lady-in-waiting,
who would often find her arms overflowing with flowers.
Later, it was the lady-in-waiting's duty to ensure that all the
bouquets were sent to local hospitals.

It had been decided that the princess should undertake
the Commonwealth Tour in place of her parents, as the king
was not strong enough for such a long, arduous journey
so soon after his recent lung operation. His left lung had
been removed following the discovery of a malignant tumor
and he had been ill for some time. At the state opening of
Parliament in November 1951, his speech had been read for
him by the lord chancellor, and his Christmas broadcast had
been recorded in small sections then edited together. Against
the advice of his doctors, on a cold morning on the last day
of January 1952, the king and the queen came to see us off
at the airport. This was the first time the king had been seen
in public since his operation, apparently having recovered.
My parents had been with him at Sandringham a few weeks
before and thought he seemed well, but I was struck by how

heartbreakingly frail he looked, the dark shadows under his eyes, his thin, white hair blowing in the bitter wind as he waved good-bye to his daughter.

It was very hard for the princess and Prince Philip to leave three-year-old Charles and eighteen-month-old Anne behind, but it would have been totally impractical to take them on such a long sea journey, with their parents flying off on constant whistle-stop tours, leaving virtually no time for them to spend together. Their grandparents and aunt were overjoyed to look after them and the prince and princess planned to send by the diplomatic bag regular tape recordings so the children could hear their voices, as well as telephoning, even though it was an unsatisfactory way of talking to such young children.

For the first stage of the journey I was the sole lady-in-waiting. The regular lady-in-waiting, Lady Palmer, had already set sail in SS *Gothic* with the main party and they were to wait for us in Mombasa, where we were to embark at the end of the visit to Kenya. I was in the company of the princess's private secretary, Lieutenant Colonel Martin Charteris. It was interesting to learn about the way in which such an ambitious tour was organized: planning had started a good twelve months earlier with detailed programs of the princess's itinerary submitted for approval, complete with exact timings, extremely important if everything was not to be thrown into total chaos. Prince Philip's private secretary, the cheerful Australian Mike Parker, who was acting as equerry to both the prince and princess, also traveled with us. He was an old shipmate of Prince Philip and was tasked with fixing any last-minute problems or running urgent messages. He would be liaising directly with the ADCs of the governors or governors-general of the countries we were visiting, and it was his responsibility to ensure that things ran smoothly day to day. The most essential member of the entourage—and very much the queen bee—was Bobo MacDonald, the princess's dresser. She had started out as the princess's nursery maid and been with her ever since. If Bobo was upset, the princess was upset, so we all took great care not to upset her.

My job as lady-in-waiting was to remain as close to the princess as possible in case I was needed to answer a query or convey a message. I was always to travel with the private secretary and the equerry in the car directly behind the royal car, and on engagements to sit or walk immediately behind the princess. I would hold her handbag if she had to present new colors to a regiment, and when she met crowds of well-wishers I was to take the bouquets that she could not hold. I was also to answer the huge amount of unofficial correspondence that would doubtless be arriving on a daily basis. If the princess were to carry out an engagement without Prince Philip, I would accompany her in the car, and if she gave a party I would greet the guests and look after them before the princess received them.

Mercifully, the chief lady clerk at Buckingham Palace was very experienced and had given us folders of letters she had already drafted according to the usual protocol—"The Princess Elizabeth desires me to thank you"—so we merely had to sign them. We had to dictate less straightforward letters before signing them, and as the numbers increased, we found ourselves having to deal with this part of the job on a day when we were not "in waiting."

When we arrived in Kenya, I was immediately struck by the smell of earth baked by the sun and the brilliant colors of the birds and flowers that at once reminded me of India. After a few days in Nairobi—a whirlwind introduction to a life of cheering children, regimental inspections, hospital and church visits, lunches, dinners, and receptions—we traveled north on bumpy roads, engulfed by clouds of red dust, to Sagana Lodge on the slopes of Mount Kenya in the Aberdare Mountains. This fishing lodge had been given to the prince and princess as a wedding present by the people of Kenya, and this was their first visit. Mike Parker and I were the only members of the royal household to accompany them. The princess and I spent the first two mornings riding a couple of reliable police horses that I had managed to secure, while Prince Philip and Mike relaxed, fishing in the nearby trout stream.

On the third evening we set off in an open jeep—the princess and I wearing khaki shirts and slacks, drawing a few comments from Mike, who was unused to seeing us in anything other than silk or cotton dresses. We were heading for Treetops, the tree-house-turned-miniature-hotel built in the fork of a huge three-hundred-year-old fig tree. Eric Sherbrooke Walker had built his now famed—and greatly enlarged—hotel over a large waterhole, the edges of which formed a natural salt lick that extended right to the foot of the tree.

It was a remote spot on the elephant migration path to Mount Kenya, and promised spectacular views of the elephants and many other splendid wild animals. The last quarter of a mile of the journey had to be made on foot down a track also used by the animals. Sherbrooke Walker was waiting as our guide, and warned us not to tread on twigs or scuff leaves and to walk in total silence, and speak only in a whisper in the event of a dire emergency. We followed him in single file, accompanied by some rather unsettling trumpeting and crashing sounds, until he stopped and pointed to a white

pillowcase—the sign for "Danger at the Waterhole"—flutter-
ing above the roof of the hotel. Sherbrooke Walker conferred
with Prince Philip, who whispered a rather hearty "No! Let's
go on!" After a moment's hesitation, Sherbrooke Walker decided to take the prince and princess on alone, indicating
that he would come back for Mike and me. As they set off
again, he waved vaguely at the rough ladders nailed to wor-
ryingly small trees every fifty yards or so and whispered that
we should climb up them if an animal appeared. "The safe
height is ten feet for rhino and buffalo but twenty feet for an
elephant," he hissed. Far from reassured by this instruction,
I turned to Mike, who whispered, "Pammy, if you have to
climb one of those things and feel someone overtaking you,
it will be me!" We decided not to take any chances.

The prince and princess safely climbed the ladder into the
tree house, despite the presence of a cow elephant standing
guard over her herd, anxiously flapping her ears just eleven
feet away behind the thinnest of hedges. African elephants are
far larger than Indian ones and cannot be tamed, and these
mountain elephants had a particularly ferocious reputation.
Luckily the wind was blowing across the clearing towards us
so no scent was being carried to her. The princess was already
busy filming, excited by the presence of such a wide variety of
magnificent creatures. She was also concerned for us, asking
what it had been like, being left behind in the bush. We left
her in no doubt as to our feelings. It was only later that we
learned that Jim Corbett, the great white hunter, was hidden
in the undergrowth with his loaded gun, protecting us not
only from the animals but also the threat of Mau-Mau guer-
rillas. We also heard that just after we left Treetops, elephants
had uprooted all the trees with ladders, including the very
ones that Mike and I had clung to so fearfully.

At the time, the house was very simple, comprising four very small bedrooms, a tiny dining room and kitchen, and an observation balcony that ran down the whole of one side. The bedrooms had been carefully prepared for us but the staff could do nothing to prevent the hilarious sight that greeted us as we looked up at the tree. Just before our arrival, baboons had stolen rolls of toilet paper from the minuscule loo and now the branches were festooned with large untidy swags of cheerful white. We didn't get much sleep that night, as there was so much to see once the moon was up. It was a thrilling sight, watching the animals arrive at the water-hole and observing the antics of the baby elephants that blew water from their trunks over the monkeys, as well as the young bull elephants enjoying a mock fight.

While we were standing in awed silence, watching the comings and goings before us, King George VI, aged just fifty-six and in the sixteenth year of his reign, died in his sleep. Earlier in the day he had been watching his guests shoot at Sandringham. He then retired to bed and suffered a coronary thrombosis. So the princess who had climbed up the ladder at Treetops came down the next day as a queen. Signals in cipher had been sent out to Kenya immediately but no one in Government House, Nairobi, could decipher them because the cipher book had been taken by the governor, who was already driving to Mombasa to bid us good-bye the following day. After little sleep at Treetops, we had driven the twenty or so miles back to Sagana Lodge, exhausted but euphoric after a magical night of big-game watching. We had a very easy morning, totally unaware of what was happening back in England. We must have been among the last people in the world to hear the news.

The king had been found dead by his valet when he went

in to call him. At 8:45 a.m. the king's principal private secretary had called his assistant in London, using the code word "Hyde Park," telling him to inform the prime minister and Queen Mary. At 10:45 a.m. the British news agencies were permitted to announce the king's death. The news did not begin to percolate into Kenya, which was ahead of Britain by three hours, until after 1:45 p.m. local time, the time that we, none the wiser, were finishing lunch. The rest of the royal party, waiting for us on board *Gothic*, were also oblivious. Lady Palmer had gone up on deck after lunch to admire the decorations on the buildings that lined Mombasa harbor. She was very puzzled when she noticed people had begun to pull them down.

After lunch, Prince Philip read the newspapers and dozed on his bed, while the princess wrote to her father, telling him about all the wonderful sights she had seen, emphasizing how much he would enjoy it here and saying she hoped he could come out in the future to see it for himself. Meanwhile, Martin Charteris was waiting in the lobby of the Outspan Hotel in Nyeri for his group to depart for Treetops, when a local reporter emerged from a telephone booth, ashen-faced. He told Martin that there was a Reuters newsflash proclaiming that the king was dead. For a moment neither man could speak—to them, as to the rest of the world, the news was totally unexpected. Then the dreadful implications of this information dawned on Martin and he jumped into the booth to telephone Buckingham Palace. Unable to get through, he rang Sagana Lodge to see whether he could get confirmation of the news from us. Mike answered the call and Martin was as usual discreet and told him that a Reuters newsflash was announcing the death of our "boss's father" and asked what we knew. When Mike had recovered he replied that we knew nothing, so Martin suggested we find a wireless.

There was indeed a portable wireless in the sitting room where Princess Elizabeth was writing and Mike crept in, managing to get it without her noticing. After a few minutes of static and frantic tuning we finally made out the faint sound of the solemn music with which the BBC had replaced all its programs. After the tolling of Big Ben, the news at last reached us from far away, the gravity of the newsreader's tone unmistakable. Mike confirmed the news to Martin and went straight in to tell Prince Philip, who lifted up his newspaper to cover his face in a gesture of despair, saying, "This will be such a blow." He then walked into the sitting room and asked his wife to come with him into the garden. Mike and I watched them on the lawn as they walked together slowly, up and down, up and down.

I knew how much the princess loved her father and how much he had adored her. When they returned, I instinctively gave her a hug but quickly, remembering that she was now queen, dropped into a deep curtsy. She remained completely calm and said simply, "I am so sorry. This means we all have to go home." When Martin arrived shortly after this, he asked her what she would like to be called. "Elizabeth, of course," she replied. "It's my name." She seemed surprised, but her father, Prince Albert, had become King George VI and her uncle David had become Edward VIII. Queen Elizabeth II, as she had now become, was the first sovereign in two hundred years to accede while abroad. In a strange parallel, she was the same age as Queen Elizabeth I had been on succession.

I couldn't believe the king had died—we had all imagined that it would be at least twenty years before the princess would succeed her father to the throne. It felt completely unreal, out here in Kenya, that the princess should now be the Queen of the United Kingdom and Northern Ireland and Head of the Commonwealth. There was, of course, business to attend to, which did distract us from the shock and grief. It was imperative that we leave as soon as possible. The new queen returned to her desk to approve telegrams that Martin had drafted to be sent to Churchill and to the governors-general of all the Commonwealth countries we were due to visit. Mike had to make arrangements for our journey back to England while I busied myself packing my case and Bobo hurriedly threw things into the princess's suitcases and John Dean, Prince Philip's valet, did the same. Of course, there was nothing suitable for mourning, so the queen had to wear a beige dress with a white hat.

The plans for our speedy return soon fell into place. Within two hours of hearing the news, we were ready to leave for Nanyuki airport, forty miles away. The queen was completely calm, and with her husband by her side, she thanked the members of staff at Sagana Lodge, presenting them each with a signed photograph. As we drove, it became obvious that the bush telegraph had gone before us. Local villagers stood outside their huts or lined the roads, calling out, *"Shauri mbaya kabisa"* ("The very worst has happened"). That such sympathy was shown as we drove through what was to become Mau-Mau territory was truly remarkable. Mike asked the press waiting at Nanyuki not to take photographs and they stood, every one of them, to attention, big box cameras at their feet in a mark of respect for the young queen's grief.

It had been decided that we should fly to Entebbe, where the royal BOAC Argonaut would meet us. As it was getting dark and the airport officials were anxious about lighting flares—the ground was as dry as tinder—we hurried onto the waiting DC-4 aircraft. We suffered a serious setback, however, when a severe electric storm erupted. Such was the force of it that the pilot of the Argonaut would not take off for London. I felt terribly sorry for the queen as she had to spend the next two hours under the gaze of officials. She managed, however, to make polite conversation with Sir Andrew Cohen, the governor of Uganda. Towards nine o'clock we were able to take off and the queen and Prince Philip retired to their cabin at the rear of the aircraft. I hoped that at last she would be able to have a good cry in his arms.

We flew through the night, stopping only to refuel in Libya. Thankfully Bobo had sent a message to her deputy on board SS *Gothic* and she had delivered a black coat, handbag, and shoes to the Argonaut so that the queen could arrive in England in mourning. She could not find a suitable hat, however, so a telegram was sent asking for one to be delivered when the plane arrived. It was late afternoon the next day when we started our descent over London, and we could soon see that a large official reception had gathered to welcome the new queen home. As we waited to disembark, I could see the prime minister, Winston Churchill, standing next to the leader of the Opposition, Clement Attlee, the Duke of Gloucester, and to my delight, my parents. The queen peered over my shoulder, looking for her private car but seeing only the huge black royal limousines that were drawn up in morbid ranks. "Oh," she said, "they have sent the hearse." And as she said this, softly and slowly, I was suddenly conscious that the private life of this twenty-five-year-old woman and that of her young husband—who would have to abandon his naval career—and those of their two small children, had come to an abrupt end. From now on, they would forever be in the public eye.

The queen left the plane first and Prince Philip followed, leaving a little gap so that the photographers could capture her alone. I was so relieved to see my parents, and in the privacy of our car, I conveyed my shock and the distress of the last few hours. Like me, they had thought that the king was getting better. We talked about the Queen Mother, who at fifty-one was now a widow, and within the space of a single day had been removed from center stage.

The king's body was lying in state at Westminster Hall and I went with my parents to pay our last respects. My father had admired the king and his sense of duty, believing him to be a shrewd man who was more aware of public opinion than his ministers. Unlike his elder brother, my father said, he had always striven to keep his finger on the public pulse. The king was buried at St. George's Chapel, Windsor, and as I looked at the three generations of queens in their black veils—Mary, the Queen Mother, and Elizabeth II standing together—I thought of how terrible their grief, so well hidden, must be.

I stayed on at Buckingham Palace for a couple of weeks to help with the thousands of letters and telegrams of condolence that the queen was receiving each and every day. Most were written not to a remote "celebrity," but to a real person who happened to be their queen, the head of a royal family that meant a great deal to them. Some came from women who had recently lost a parent and wanted to empathize with her situation. Many of the stories we read were deeply moving and they showed how widely the late king had been revered. These letters were a source of great comfort to the queen.

Not all of the authors of these letters were quite so

balanced, and among the piles organized under the collective headings of "children," "women," and "service families," we also had "lunatics." We spent hours opening, reading, sorting, and replying to them all. One afternoon six of us were sitting in a circle on the floor going through the post when I opened a telegram that was signed "Mama in Chicago." "Oh, listen to this!" I cried, delighted at a diversion from our sad task. "One for the lunatic pile!" Unbeknownst to me, the queen had just entered the room and my laughter was met by stony silence. "Pammy," she said, "Mama is in Chicago just now." As she removed the telegram from my hand I remembered, to my horror, that Aunt Alice, Prince Philip's mother, was indeed in Chicago, raising money for her religious order. We continued our work in silence.

I had only been asked to be a lady-in-waiting for the Commonwealth Tour, which had now been postponed, so I went to Malta to join my parents. My father was now commander in chief of the Mediterranean Fleet, a job he had very much desired. The proprietor of the *Daily Express*, Lord Beaverbrook, however, was still running his campaign to turn the public against my father. This vendetta had started when the film *In Which We Serve* opened with a shot of the *Daily Express* floating in the water, boasting the headline "No War This Year." It was dated 1 September 1939, two days before the declaration of war. Beaverbrook had been a great champion of my father when he was made the young chief of Combined Operations, but when my father asserted his independence from "the Beaver" this was not forgiven. There may also have been another reason why Beaverbrook pursued this vendetta. In the 1930s Max's mistress, Jean Norton, was my mother's best friend. Jeanie and my father liked to go riding—she was an excellent horsewoman and he thought she had the perfect figure for a woman on a horse. But while they enjoyed riding together they were never lovers, as Max possibly suspected. When the *Daily Mirror* columnist Bill Connor, aka "Cassandra," arrived in Malta, he told my father over lunch that Lord Beaverbrook had sent him out to "report on the riots." "But there are no riots in Malta," Bill had replied. "Then start some," Lord Beaverbrook had roared. At the beginning of the Second World War Cassandra had to cease his famous column because of paper shortages. When peace was declared it started again with the words, "As I was saying before I was so rudely interrupted . . ."

We now lived in Admiralty House in Valletta. In the entrance hall the soaring staircase rose between great marble plaques that listed all the naval commanders in chief since Nelson. The garden overlooked the ramparts and could be reached only through a tunnel beneath the street and a climb up a steep staircase. When the fleet was berthed in Malta my father worked in an office overlooking Grand Harbour.

When Aunt Louise and Uncle Gustav of Sweden came to visit us, it was touching to see my father reminisce with his sister about their time spent on the island as children. While returning from a day out visiting their old haunts, however, driving along the Sliema harbor front, my father—a notoriously bad driver—managed to overturn the car, much to the horror of my mother, Uncle Gustav, and me, who were in the car behind. Fortunately Aunt Louise and my father scrambled out unhurt, but the car lay rather helplessly upside down by the side of the road. As torrid newspaper headlines ran through our minds, a troop of Royal Marines came into view. Seeing his commander in chief standing at the roadside, their commanding officer brought them smartly to a halt and saluted. "Ah, Captain Huntingford," said my father, "oblige me by righting my car." And with a heave-ho, the Royal Marines obliged him and we were soon back on the road.

Ever more adventurous and keen to see different parts of the world, I went to stay with George Arida—a dashing young Lebanese man whom I had first met during our previous time in Malta—and his family in their apartment in Beirut as well as their little house in the mountains, "the Cedars." It was very beautiful up there with astonishing vistas, and surrounded by the cedars from which, it was said, King Solomon had built his temple. We spent our days waterskiing and our evenings socializing with the Paris-chic Lebanese women and their husbands, including George's attractive sister Jacqueline, who was married to the son of the president of Lebanon. These were heady days and it wasn't long before George and I fell for each other. I had had a couple of romances previously but had never really been in love. George was shy and quiet but a romantic, sweet-natured man, and if circumstances had been different, we would have been inseparable. We always found our partings distressing and were consoled only by the constant stream of love letters that followed.

Such was the depth of my feelings for George and our desire to see each other as often as we could that I chose to follow my heart and not accompany my mother on a trip to Delhi to see Panditji. He teased me in a subsequent letter: "It's been a joy to have your mother here, when you have deserted us and not come this way." But I could tell he was pleased that I was happy and I knew that I would be seeing him later that year for, some sixteen months after the death of King George VI, the queen's coronation was due to take place. While the queen had indeed been declared sovereign the moment her father had died on 6 February 1952, it had taken sixteen months to organize the coronation. As tradition declared that the monarch has to be crowned in sight of "all of the people," a great many heads of state from all over the world had been invited to attend. Of course, this had a knock-on effect as the seating capacity inside Westminster Abbey had to be pretty much expanded threefold to accommodate the eight thousand or so guests. There had been some concern that the death of the queen's grandmother on 24 April, just a few weeks before the coronation, would mean that it would have to be postponed, but Queen Mary had thoughtfully made known her desire that no one must be in mourning during the coronation.

And so, on 2 June 1953, the world witnessed the most public of coronations. To begin with, it was the first time that television cameras had been allowed inside Westminster Abbey and it was also the first time that a great event had been broadcast live throughout the nation. An estimated forty million people across the world would be able to watch it on television in addition to another eleven million who would listen in on the wireless. As such there were many rehearsals before the great day, the Duchess of Norfolk deputizing for the queen, though Queen Elizabeth did have to practice wearing the crown the day before as the St. Stephen's Crown weighed a colossal seven pounds. Anne Glenconner later told me that she and the other maids of honor had to keep putting the brakes on when they walked behind the queen carrying her train to avoid running into each other, as everything was so much slower than they had rehearsed it.

The more than eight thousand guests in attendance included royalty and dignitaries from all over the world. Every crowned head was given a carriage in which to arrive at the abbey, and as there were so many people to get in, several peers processed to their seats with sandwiches concealed beneath their coronets. My mother, Patricia, John, and I had been instructed by the lord chamberlain to arrive only an hour before the ceremony began so we did not have too long to wait. My father had a rather unsettling ride behind the coronation coach, on a horse that was so fresh it pranced around and would not keep to a dignified walk. When he dismounted at the abbey and the Life Guard trooper approached to take the reins, my father told him, somewhat tetchily—and unrealistically—to take the horse away and exercise it.

The queen was dressed in a white satin gown designed for her by Norman Hartnell. The full skirt was embroidered with beaded emblems of the United Kingdom and all the Commonwealth countries, including a rose, a thistle, a shamrock, a maple leaf, a fern, and the lotus flower of India picked out in diamante and seed pearls. This dress had taken over three thousand hours of handiwork to complete. As she processed into the abbey, her long crimson velvet train was borne by her six maids of honor, their stunning dresses completing the tableau. The whole effect was magical.

I knew that, for the queen, the coronation ceremony meant a great deal, particularly the anointing, for which she had requested the cameras be turned off. This was the most moving part of the rite, and when it came, the maids of honor stepped forward to take her velvet robes and jewelry. When they then covered her coronation dress with the simple white linen overdress, I was struck by how young, vulnerable, and alone the queen appeared. There was a hushed stillness, a sense of gravity and occasion, as the Archbishop of Canterbury anointed her hands, her head, and her heart with the consecrated oil that symbolized her divine right to rule. And while she may have looked fragile, the certainty in her voice as she said her vows was inspiring. During the investiture, the lord chamberlain presented her with golden spurs, the symbol of chivalry, after which the archbishop offered a jeweled sword and armills, golden bracelets denoting sincerity and wisdom. Then the Imperial Mantle, the gold royal robe that had been used by her father in his coronation, was placed over the white linen robe and she received the orb, the coronation ring, the glove, and the scepter. As the new queen was crowned, the abbey resounded with the dramatic and thunderous acclamations of "Long Live the Queen!" and "God Save the Queen!"

Prince Philip was the first to do obeisance to her, bowing and kissing her cheek. His mother, Aunt Alice, led the royal family's procession out of the abbey towards the West Door amid the glorious music that echoed round the nave. I was so used to seeing her dressed in a workaday gray jacket and skirt and short nun's veil—she had founded a nursing order of Greek Orthodox nuns in 1949, modeled on the convent set up by my great-aunt Ella, Grand Duchess Elizabeth of Russia—that it was a surprise to see her looking so dignified and regal in her finely woven floor-length woolen cloak and flowing veil.

During the procession back to Buckingham Palace, the queen wore the newly made velvet purple Robe of State, edged with ermine and embroidered around the border in gold, the work of twelve seamstresses from the Royal School of Needlework. The route to the palace had been designed so that as many people as possible could see the queen, and because of the large number of people taking part—just under thirty thousand officers, not to mention the vast number of royals from all over the world—it was three kilometers long and took two hours to complete. The Queen of Tonga won the hearts of the public by not putting up the cover over her carriage, despite the rain. But what sent the press into overdrive was Princess Margaret's gesture of brushing a piece of lint from the jacket of Captain Peter Townsend, the late queen's equerry and a divorced man.

Following the procession, the queen came out onto the balcony of the palace to wave to the crowds and watch the flypast. In the evening, as "the lights of London" came on all the way down the Mall, to the National Gallery, and down to the Tower of London, we watched the firework display with Panditji. He took a seat next to my mother, with my father on the other side, and I sat behind them. It soon became clear that the people sitting next to me did not realize my connection, for a woman behind me exclaimed to her neighbor, "Golly, look—there is Lady Mountbatten. And that's the Indian Nehru next to her. How *can* she let him sit so near?" At that moment, Nehru, in the familiar way he had with everyone, put his hand on my mother's arm to point something out. The effect on the couple behind me was immediate: "Look, he is touching her. How *can* she let him? It's disgusting." Hearing this sent a shiver down my spine.

I listened intently that evening as the queen made a speech to her subjects around the world, speaking of her wish to unite her people. When she said, "I have in sincerity pledged myself to your service, as so many of you are pledged to mine. Throughout my life and with all my heart I shall strive to be worthy of your trust. In this resolve I have my husband to support me. He shares my ideals and my affection for you," I knew this to be true.

## 16

The Commonwealth Tour was to resume in early November 1953. Once again I was not happy at the thought of going away for nearly six months as I was still very much in love with George and wanted to see him as much as possible. I had a sense that my parents were relieved I was going away, for while they liked George, they felt I wouldn't be happy living in Lebanon. My mother thought he was a "sweet man with impeccable manners," but my father teased me that George always wore fingerless leather gloves for waterskiing and a similar pair for driving and he was puzzled by the fact that George always dressed entirely in black. It would be even longer than usual before George and I could meet again. We were used to writing long, detailed, intimate letters and I consoled myself that, so far, our feelings for each other had not been changed by spending so much time apart. He was such a romantic, but after I refused another of his marriage proposals he ended one of his letters by saying that I had a "pumping machine instead of a heart." I was somewhat affronted but it soon became a joke between us.

I had to prepare for the tour, and while this time I already had a wardrobe full of dresses, bags, hats, and gloves, now that the princess was queen, the whole thing was on a much grander scale. Henriette had remarried, so the other lady-in-waiting was to be Lady Alice Egerton, whom I knew from Malta. We were to take turns at being in attendance unless we were both required for very formal occasions such as the opening of Parliament. I liked Alice, who I knew would be a caustic and amusing companion, but I still felt forlorn and lonely at the prospect of the tour and was grateful to Patricia for coming down to the King George V Dock to see me off. This time I was not flying out to Bermuda and going on to Jamaica with the queen and Prince Philip but instead was part of the advance party sailing out on board SS *Gothic*. As soon as I embarked I could see that the party on board *Gothic* consisted of several senior members of the royal household I scarcely knew and an atmosphere redolent of Buckingham Palace prevailed. This time we would be in the presence of Sir Michael Adeane, the queen's private secretary, who held the same rank as a cabinet minister. Martin Charteris, her assistant private secretary, was flying out to Bermuda with her. It was a bit like the first day at a new school, and I was once again filled with dread at the prospect of being away for so long. I decided to hide in my cabin until we left the dock, but as it turned out, owing to the presence of the formidable Miss Bramford, this unsettled me even more.

Miss Bramford was to be my lady's maid, inherited from a previous lady-in-waiting. I had never had a lady's maid but had been told that it was essential for the tour because of the crowded program of official events, timed to the minute, that required many changes of clothing, with no time for packing, unpacking, ironing crumpled dresses, or finding the appropriate accessories. Miss Bramford was small, late-middle-aged and extremely well spoken, and I was immediately intimidated by her presence as she bustled around my cabin. I went up on deck, where, shivering and homesick already, I had a strong urge to jump ashore and take the first plane out to Malta or Ethiopia, where my parents were visiting Emperor Haile Selassie with the Mediterranean Fleet. When Admiral Sir Conolly Abel Smith came to tell me that my father had sent a lovely farewell signal, I wobbled all over again.

Going out of the dock through the lock into the mouth of the Thames took us over an hour. The passage was so narrow that from the center of the deck you couldn't see the water at all, which gave the disconcerting impression of sailing over land. Our departure was neither romantic nor impressive. The water was dirty and the docks were deserted, bleak, and cold, the scene made all the more desolate by a knot of five or six children who had come with their parents to wave us off. They stood forlornly huddled, together with a photographer whose occasional flash lit up the dirt and drabness of the dock. I waved with as much enthusiasm as I could muster, though not terribly heartily, I am sorry to say. It was only when we passed through and the surrounding lights played on the water that the outline of the docks began to look rather lovely. I went down below, hoping that Miss Bramford had retired to bed.

We were to be at sea for a fortnight before meeting up with the rest of our party, and this certainly gave everyone on board *Gothic* a chance to get to know each other. I found that the senior members of the royal household were much less pompous and intimidating than they had at first appeared. Apart from members of the royal household, those on board consisted of the Royal Navy party (of which Conolly was in charge); the officers and crew of *Gothic*; and the press party, an essential element of the tour's PR. There were six senior press representatives on board for the trip to Jamaica, including my old friends from the previous tour, John Turner, the newsreel cameraman, and the very tall broadcast journalist Godfrey Talbot—he of the very British voice. It soon became clear that they all shared a lively passion for taking photographs and they were endlessly pursuing us around the deck with their Brownies and color film cameras, which became somewhat tiresome. But all in all they were a great team, and contributed an enormous amount of fun to the general melee.

It took me a while to find my sea legs, but by the third day we had all begun to engage in tremendous bouts of deck tennis, quoits, and deck croquet, which we played with wooden blocks instead of balls. In the afternoons, there were terrific canasta sessions, at which I was rather good, and also liar dice, at which I was extraordinarily bad. Nearly every night there was a cocktail party before dinner. And so, as our so-called relaxed program continued, I began to believe—incorrectly as it turned out—that the *actual* program of the tour would come as a rest cure.

During the second week, I spent much of the time impersonating the queen. As regular worship was an important part of the royal couple's life, it was felt that we should rehearse a church service—as well as several other types of occasion—and for this I was asked to represent the queen. Unfortunately, as we took up our positions, the ship lurched sideways and I couldn't make up my mind whether "the queen" should stand firmly with her feet wide apart during the national anthem or stand with her feet together and risk falling over. To begin with, Jeremy Hall, the naval equerry from New Zealand, stood in for Prince Philip, but he reduced me to helpless giggles and nobody could take the rehearsal seriously. The next time, my old friend Mike Cowan, the queen's Australian equerry, stood in for the prince and he made sure everyone took it seriously, and two unsuspecting stand-ins and the stills photographer were made to do deep bows when presented to me. The rehearsals turned out to be a good idea, as none of the stewards knew how to deal with a formal dinner party. Oulton, the sergeant footman, watched as we staged a mock party, hissing instructions from the wings and making us feel as though we were actors in a rather bad play.

We arrived in Jamaica twelve days after leaving London. In the light of dawn, Kingston harbor was a remarkable sight—a narrow stretch of sand and grass lay beyond the water and very steep hills, covered in dense vegetation, rose up dramatically behind. I had imagined Kingston to be a sprawling city, so was surprised to discover that it was nothing more than a shantytown consisting of a couple of long main streets. Coming ashore, I was a little apprehensive as the governor, Sir Hugh Foot, had signaled to the ship some days earlier to say that as soon as we landed he wanted to "kidnap" Johnny Althorp, the queen's equerry, and me, and take us to King's House for discussions with him and Lady Foot. Arriving at the house, I was stopped in my tracks by the beauty of its setting—the lawns were a vibrant green following the rainy season, and the flower beds were vivid with pink and white bougainvillea, red poinsettia, and the many colors of cannas. At the end of the garden, beyond the Royal Cotton tree—so called because of its immense size—was a superb view of the foothills of the Blue Mountains.

The governor and Lady Foot—mischievously nicknamed "the Feet" by Princess Margaret on a previous visit—had pushed Jamaica into a complete state of panic. Preparations for the tour had been going on for the past nine months and there had been intensive rehearsals for every single function. Now our arrival had thrown everyone into ecstasies of excitement, and with a heavy sense of doom, Johnny and I realized that we were to be seized and "rehearsed with" throughout our stay.

Lady Foot was charming but imperious. As soon as I arrived she took me on a tour of inspection of the house, as the queen and Prince Philip would be staying with her and her husband. The layout was so simple that even I, who always managed to get myself lost, felt confident I had committed it to memory, and yet Lady Foot told me to retrace my steps to ensure that I knew every corner. Minutes later, she informed me how many times a day the queen would be changing her dress. When I assured her that the queen would have no intention of changing three times in one morning, she was driven to exclaim, "But we can't have a crumpled queen!" Lady Foot then took me to the queen's bedroom and asked whether it was correct for the governor's wife to show the queen into her bedroom or whether she must remain on the threshold and so presumably shout out directions as to the geography of the room from a distance. I tried to indicate that formality should not outweigh practicality, but she obviously felt that no detail was too small to discuss. This, then, was my initiation into the strange behavior, or the total loss of common sense, that occurs during a royal tour. I had been warned by the other, more experienced members of the party that often people went into complete overdrive.

The governor came from an influential left-wing family—his brother was the Labour MP Michael Foot—and he was a charismatic man, with a progressive attitude. After my experiences in India, it was refreshing to hear him say that it never occurred to either the white or black inhabitants of the island that parties should not be mixed. I found him fascinating to talk to; nevertheless, after a day's conscientious observance of the Foots' enthusiastic rehearsal schedule, I made a bold bid for freedom, asking the governor to lend Conolly and me two ponies. He was somewhat shocked that I should want to ride "at a time like this" but he acquiesced. Being used to my own company, I desperately needed to escape from all the people and overwhelming preparations, and as the admiral and I rode through the grounds of King's House, around two enormous fields of waist-high grasses, I began to feel calmer. My pony was called Admiral and the admiral's pony was Sailor Boy, something I found infinitely funnier than he did. Conolly had taken it upon himself to stand in loco parentis for me, which was touching but also somewhat frustrating. Once he knew that I would be arriving back on board *Gothic* after him following a night out in Kingston, he told Commander Colin Madden to send a boat back to shore to wait for me. Colin had passed the order on to the officer of the watch, adding, "When Lady Pamela comes on board, tell her that she's a damn nuisance and I'm very angry." The officer of the watch that night happened to be the sixth officer, the baby of the party. No sooner had I stepped on board than he came up and with a tremendous salute took a deep breath and said, "Ma'am. Commander Madden says that you're a damned nuisance and he's very angry. Thank you, ma'am."

The queen and Prince Philip arrived and I took over from Alice. The program was intense and, of course, run with military precision by Lady Foot, who had produced a forty-three-page booklet of timings, instructions, and endless lists of the people we were due to meet. She seemed to have memorized everything and later, when Alice took out her booklet to check someone's name, Lady Foot looked at her aghast, exclaiming, "What! You don't know it?"

As we drove through the streets of Kingston it was as if the whole of Jamaica had turned out to greet the queen and Prince Philip. I traveled in the second open car with the governor and Lady Foot, and the one word you could hear being passed from mouth to mouth was "Sweet!" "Sweet!" The men, it had to be said, were somewhat less excited than the women, who jumped up and down, dancing round and round in circles. I hoped the queen would be able to see some of Jamaica's natural beauty—the banana groves, the endless sugarcane covered in pink flowers, the tall, slender royal palms—as the streets of Kingston had been festooned with so much royal bunting, it was impossible to see what anything really looked like. At a rally for over forty thousand school-children, I stood next to the immensely tall Chief Minister Bustamante—known as Busta—and as I opened my mouth to remark on how proud he must be, he turned to me and with a huge smile exclaimed, "We are unbeatable!"

The rest of the Jamaican tour was enjoyable and fault-lessly precise in its organization and logistics. Even Lady Foot, however, could not have anticipated the scenario at our last event—an inspection of a guard of honor in Port Royal. When it was over, as the queen was making her way to the barge, a man ducked out from under the barrier and threw his white jacket on the ground before her. Actually it missed one of the numerous puddles on the ground but, entering into the spirit, the queen went to step on it when Brigadier Jackson, the garrison commander, dragged it out of the way and hurled the man back into the arms of the police. Later, we were astonished to hear that the man, Warren Kidd, had been arrested on charges of lunacy. However we later learned that he had been found sane by a doctor and was subsequently released.

By the time we came to leave I was looking forward to a few days off, as Alice was due to take over duties in Panama. I also wanted to stay on board *Gothic* as she went through the canal. Alice was struck down by heart palpitations, however, and I had to resign myself to being on duty throughout Panama, a prospect not lightened by the fact that Mike Cowan was the equerry. He appeared to rely on me for an understanding of the royal duties and protocol, unlike Johnny, whose experience I had been able to rely on during our stay in Jamaica.

Panama proved to be quite a trial, the crowds behaving very differently from those in Jamaica. As we drove through the spacious streets of Cristóbal, an unenthusiastic group of Americans stood around looking as if they would rather be anywhere else, but then as we left the Canal Zone and entered the city of Colón, a large crowd of people appeared, yelling itself hoarse, and intent, it seemed, on thrusting themselves into our car. We were being accompanied on foot by some rather overweight policemen who walked at such a slow pace that this soon became an invitation for the crowds to break rank and swarm around our vehicles. With much hooting of horns, our drivers tried to increase their speed, and the fat policemen broke into a run, their hands feverishly clutching their revolvers. One policeman decided to take out a vicious-looking whip and began to lay into the crowd. By this point Michael and I had become separated from the queen and Prince Philip's car by a sea of bodies. It was rather frightening and we were particularly concerned for the safety of those who kept running into the path of our car. The drivers narrowly managed to avoid running anybody down, however, and we decamped outside the town hall—unnerved, and hot and bothered by the unpleasant humidity.

A band played something that might have been "God Save the Queen" and, with far more gusto, the Panamanian national anthem, then on the steps of the town hall the mayor presented the queen with a gold key to the city. Where was Lady Foot when we needed her? As we fought our way past ranks of Girl Guides, I went to take the key from the queen and for the first time she seemed quite lost and bewildered. Not wishing to impale myself on the bayonets of the soldiers, I found myself climbing over a row of parked motorcycles and in so doing getting oil all over a very smart new dress. The industrious Miss Bramford certainly had her work cut out that evening. Meanwhile, Johnny Althorp had became entangled in the band. Each time he tried to escape, the trombone players extended their slides and trapped him.

We drove back out of Colón to the Canal Zone, where American outriders accompanied us some thirty miles to a lock in the canal. The vegetation was deep green, thick and swampy, and the atmosphere oppressive, and I couldn't help thinking of the thousands of lives sacrificed for the building of the canal. Having watched a Panamanian ship go through the lock, we were taken for lunch with the governor, who expressed surprise that we hadn't already sailed on *Gothic* along the canal, as this was by far the best way to see it. We bit our lips to stop ourselves pointing out that it was his wretched lunch party that was preventing us from doing so. After the reception, we were thankfully able to return to *Gothic*, hoping for the merest glimpse as she passed through the canal. It turned out, however, that we were not allowed up on deck because it was a Sunday and we hadn't yet been to church. The American bishop, Gooden, insisted on coming on board and holding a service belowdecks, in the day cabin. We got our revenge by looking out of the window the whole time.

That evening we had an official dinner at the presidential palace, followed by a reception elsewhere. Michael and I were nervous, not at all happy if the queen and Prince Philip were out of our sight, and when they were driven off from the palace after dinner, leaving us behind, Michael pushed me into a luxurious limousine, pointed in anguish at the queen's departing car, and commanded the driver to "Follow that car." The chauffeur protested that the car we had jumped into belonged to the president of the Legislative Assembly, but Michael was insistent. Later, at the reception, I found myself sitting next to the president of the Assembly, who said mutinously, "You stole my car." I offered profuse apologies and muttered something about not knowing it was his car. But he had not finished and a twinkle appeared in his eye. "You stole my car, so I stole the foreign minister's car. The foreign minister stole the chancellor's car, and the chancellor had to hail a taxi." The chancellor, it appeared, was not one to bear a grudge lightly and, white with rage, sat in stony silence for the rest of the evening, refusing to speak to anyone.

It was a joy to set sail in *Gothic* knowing we had sixteen days at sea before we reached Fiji. It was good to have the queen and Prince Philip on board, and we became gloriously busy, not achieving a great deal, but enjoying ourselves immensely. We soon all became addicted to deck croquet, the outcome of which depended on how much the ship was rolling and how recently the decks had been washed down. We had played quite sedately on our journey out to Jamaica but now that he was here, Prince Philip was having none of that, introducing us instead to deck hockey "minus rules." Within thirty seconds of the first game, the *Exchange Telegraph* correspondent was flat on his back and he was still having medical treatment after we arrived in New Zealand. By the time we reached Fiji there were four sprained ankles, four seriously crushed fingers, and countless minor injuries, but as Prince Philip always managed to come out quite unscathed, the games continued until the day we came ashore. Commander Derek Steele-Perkins, the queen's doctor, was the referee, but the only time he ever blew the whistle was at the end of a period, and he invariably turned a completely deaf medical ear to the screams of agony when someone was hit harder than usual. I had been a keen player on our way out from England, winning the championship partnered by *Gothic*'s first officer, Andy Anderson, but I now decided it would be much safer to be an enthusiastic onlooker.

On 4 December we crossed the equator. Alice and I had thought we were going to get away without a "crossing the line" ceremony, but with Prince Philip on board this was unlikely. Wildly enthused, he set about establishing his court, appointing his King Neptune, Queen Ariadne, and other members of the court. The victims were Alice and me, two of the Wrens, and a few of the female clerks. The court was held on a platform erected above the swimming pool on the forward deck. The ship's officers and all of our party lined the rails overlooking it and the sailors, marines, cooks, and stewards packed the deck surrounding the platform. To make matters worse, Godfrey Talbot was recording the proceedings for the BBC, John Turner and his newsreel cameras were suspended above us, and the *Times* photographer was clearly visible among the crowd. The ceremony got off to a good start when Neptune fell into the pool and the public prosecutor announced that he was in his element. The charges were read and I was accused of being late for breakfast, having for a father a sea lord and admiral not appointed by King Neptune, being a disturbing influence in the ship, and reminding the prosecutor of one of his favorite mermaids. I was made to sit in a chair and given something to hold by Prince Philip while lather was slapped all over me. I was so busy squirming around to avoid the various horrors that it was some time before I realized I was holding an enormous wet fish, the greatest horror of all. Prince Philip said, "You don't mind going in backwards, do you?" and all of a sudden tipped the chair, flinging me backwards into the pool. As I surfaced, "the bears," all arrayed in soggy skirts, grabbed me and, having been assured I was all right, promptly ducked me under again. The same had happened to Alice and everyone watching had been so convinced that we would have our necks broken that all the other victims were merely thrown into the pool sideways. The fact that most of the victims couldn't swim just added to the general excitement. When it was over a free-for-all broke out among the court, all of whom ended up in the pool, together with pots of paint, beef bones, cabbages, my fish, and the various robes that King Neptune had discarded. Having been aghast at the idea of the ceremony, I actually ended up having enormous fun, but the queen hated every minute of it because from where she was sitting it really did look as if we were all going to drown.

Our arrival in Fiji could not have been livelier. Coming into Suva harbor, we were surrounded by a number of brightly decorated little yachts, and then, to my huge delight, a dozen outriggers appeared, each sailed by a crew of Fijians in grass skirts. I had never seen canoes such as these before, each one having been cut from a single log with the outrigger secured by lashings of coconut fiber. I was told that most of them had sailed from the Lau group of islands, some two hundred miles away. When we had anchored, five chiefs from Bau and Rewa came on board the *Gothic* to perform the "Cavuikelekele," an invitation to land. I was on deck when Conolly received them. He introduced me but then expected me to cope. The men were enormous, and their skirts and upper clothing of bark cloth and leaves made them seem even more so. They appeared to speak no English, so after brightly gesticulating towards the outriggers and various points in the harbor with appreciative and inquiring noises, I finally succumbed to silence. I was startled when some minutes later the largest of them fixed me with a steely look and said, "The chiefs would like to sit. They are not accustomed to standing." Unable to decide whether we had committed a serious breach of etiquette or whether they were protesting against the physical exertion, Conolly and I looked at each other in panic. There were no available chairs, the main deck was already packed with spectators and press, the band was still on parade, and people were tearing round in all directions in the remaining few minutes before the queen and Prince Philip and the governor and his wife were due to come up on deck. Conolly finally indicated a portion of the deck where only the people coming down from the upper deck would trip over them, and they squatted there quite happily.

The welcoming ceremony was spectacular. The queen sat on a small platform in the middle of the deck, the governor and Prince Philip on either side of her, with the Fijian intercedent—the *matanivanua*—squatting at her feet. The chiefs came towards her on their knees, not without some difficulty as their skirts kept getting in the way, and when the other chiefs stopped, the most senior came forward and presented a whale's tooth hung with sennit cord. The queen

accepted this *tabua*—the most highly prized article of traditional Fijian property—and passed it to the *matanivanua*,
who made a formal speech of acceptance on her behalf. The
senior chief then backed away to rejoin the others, and after
three or four slow, hollow claps with cupped palms, they all
backed away, still on their knees.

This was all carried out in silence as the Fijians considered it disrespectful to make any noise during formal ceremonies. We learned quickly that although the Fijians often
looked very fierce, everything they did was carried out with
enormous dignity. This also meant that Fijian obeisance ritu-
als were very long. At one point Prince Philip tried shaking
hands while the chiefs were sitting down, having done their
three claps to the queen, to avoid their having to repeat the
ritual all over again to him, but he merely put them off their
stride so that they had to start counting their claps all over
again.

Two days later we took off in a flying boat bound for
Tonga, arriving two and a half hours later, at noon, to find
that Tonga time was nicely original, being twenty minutes
ahead of Fiji time and twelve hours and twenty minutes
ahead of GMT. Tonga interested me—I was astonished to
read in the brief that there was no fresh running water anywhere on the islands, but it was admirable to think that there
was one hundred percent literacy among the population
owing to compulsory education. We were off to the small
town of Nuku'alofa, as guests of Queen Salote, whose father, King George II, had placed Tonga under British protection in 1900 while maintaining its status as a self-governing
state. Although Britain controlled the country's finances, it
was otherwise completely independent, a typical greeting to
outsiders being "Tonga is still Tonga!"

Queen Salote had endeared herself to the British during the coronation, and it was easy to see why she was so loved by her people. She was held in great respect, as a leader, an orator, a poet, and a composer, her songs sung on even the most remote islands. She embodied the spirit of Tonga, where song and dance were part of the everyday life of the people. She understood her subjects and astonishingly knew most of them personally—they numbered around fifty thousand. A special respectful language was used to address the queen; another was used for people of chiefly rank, and the ordinary language was spoken only between people of equal rank. Salote was regarded as the ultimate authority on all questions of rank, precedence, and custom, having an outstanding knowledge of Tongan genealogies. It was an extremely stratified society—your status was determined at birth and your achievements could do little to alter it, yet the social position of women was extremely high, sisters always outranking brothers within the family, the person deciding important questions such as marriage being the father's sister. It was forbidden to pass in front of a person of higher rank, and because Tongans had to ensure that their heads were at a lower height than anyone of greater rank, we often saw people rushing about bent double. It was fortunate that Salote was so tall and that her sons were only a couple of inches shorter. Her sons were remarkably robust young men, each weighing over twenty-four stone—your weight and bearing being a sign of how well-off and high up the social scale you were.

It was a noisy arrival. The queen's first engagement was to inspect the Royal Guard drawn up on the wharf. The route was packed, and for a while each group cheered on a single long-drawn-out note, and as the pitch for each group was different, the effect was harmonious. The controlled cheering soon deteriorated into shrill yelling, however, which was deafening, and it continued without break until we reached the palace.

The palace was a small wooden house painted white with a dark-red corrugated-iron roof. A large and sumptuous bathroom had been specially installed for the visit. Queen Salote and her entire family had moved out so that the queen, Prince Philip, Mike Cowan, and I could stay there. They had left the many members of staff, however. My room was tiny, a walled-off passage but with a particularly comfortable bed. The fact that two sides of the room were composed entirely of windows made dressing and undressing difficult. Each window had tiny net curtains attached and you could either shut the windows and die of heat or open them and change in view of the whole of Nuku'alofa. As the garden was very small and the wall separating us from the street and neighboring buildings was only three feet high, everyone had congregated just beneath my room, cheering and waving whenever I went into it. They thought it great fun when I brushed my hair, so I opted for the heat, changing and sleeping in a hermetically sealed oven.

A feast was given for an astonishing seven hundred people, all seated cross-legged on cushions. The food was bountiful—roast suckling pig, crayfish, yams, chicken, breadfruit, watermelons, pineapples, and coconut—the freshest and most delicious food we had eaten so far on the tour. There were no implements of any kind and small girls dressed in white knelt nearby waving little fly whisks every time the insects tried to settle on our food. The Tongan serving women carved out endless and generous portions of food and handed them over on leaves. I was soon surrounded by a mountain of leaves and hardly knew whether to be embarrassed or proud. The queen gallantly did the best her small appetite would allow and was able to spin it out for some time, knowing that as the person of highest rank, when she stopped eating, everyone else would also have to put down their leaves.

This was a royal visit with a difference, all aspects of our daily routine seemingly on show. Later that evening, intending to make my way over to the bathroom, I found so many prostrate bodies sleeping on the staircase and in passages that the only means of getting to the bathroom was through Mike's room. I bumped into the queen, who was also tiptoeing through Mike's room. When she turned on the light in the bathroom she found that its other door had been thrown open to the garden and that she was now in full view of the town and the four hundred or so men who were sitting around campfires in the garden. Even the next morning, a Sunday, when we had hoped to have a bit of a lie-in, the queen and Prince Philip were woken at dawn by four men blowing nose flutes in their honor.

Before we left we were presented with grass skirts and garlands. The men put theirs on rather willingly—and were immediately transformed—and we were amused to note that the admiral was particularly gifted in the hula motion of the hips. Rather more reserved, we women wore our garlands but carried our grass skirts over our arms. As we said good-bye, Queen Salote had tears running down her cheeks, and while we settled ourselves in *Gothic*, she and her family sailed five miles out to sea so that they could wave to us as we passed. We took with us the memory of a surprisingly shy woman who possessed enormous talent, charm, and ability, and an island whose people had given us a welcome and hospitality that we would never forget.

It was approaching Christmas, and as we knew we wouldn't get a chance to celebrate properly once the New Zealand leg began, we had a crazy festive dinner party. Prince Philip excelled himself, managing to use three cracker blowers at once—one in his mouth and one up each nostril, the shiny rolls unraveling simultaneously. On 23 December, as we docked in Auckland, the more formal part of the royal tour began. This was also when the private secretaries took over the schedule, each moment timed to within a second of its existence, and what better start, I thought, than the governor-general and his wife, who were allocated precisely three minutes on board. There was a busy schedule ahead of us in New Zealand; even Christmas Eve was to be spent on duty. The morning of Christmas Eve was spent at Auckland Hospital, but the populace was apparently so healthy, there had been a certain amount of difficulty filling it up for the visit. In the afternoon the queen addressed a crowd of children, which later, in private, she said was a waste of time for the poor children as her speech had been so pompous.

Then tragically, on Christmas Day, there was a terrible rail disaster, the worst in New Zealand's history. The night express from Wellington to Auckland crashed through a weakened bridge spanning a river swollen by floodwater at Tangiwai. Prince Philip accompanied the prime minister to Wellington to attend the funeral of the victims. The mood was subdued as the queen made her Christmas broadcast, and being so far from our families made us all a bit miserable. I thought of my parents, my sister, my nephews, and John as the queen said, "Of course we all want our children at Christmastime—for that is the season above all when each family gathers at its own hearth. I hope that perhaps mine are listening to me now." I realized how difficult it was for her to be apart from her children for so long.

By this point in the tour, I had resigned myself to the repetition of ceremonies. The public welcomes lasted only fifteen minutes, consisting of the national anthem, the presentation of a bouquet, followed by a gift from the town, the presentation of the town council and local dignitaries, the signing of the town hall visitors' book, and lastly the hip-hooraying or three cheers. The welcome had been excellently devised to keep the queen and Prince Philip occupied so that everybody could gaze at them for a quarter of an hour. A civic reception was the same, with the addition of an address by the mayor and a reply by the queen, and so lasted around twenty minutes. Everything was formulaic by necessity, and I would find myself looking for something to distract me such as the entry of an inevitable stray dog or someone's hat blowing off. Prince Philip always acted as master of ceremonies, prompting the mayor with "Would you like to present your councillors?" And if both the mayor and the town clerk forgot, he would ask, "And are you going to have three cheers?"

One of the strangest phenomena we noticed was crowd laughter. Whenever Prince Philip, or sometimes the queen, tried to make the ceremony a little more human by talking to one of the people being presented, the crowd would go into shrieks of laughter. It wasn't as if Prince Philip had said anything particularly funny—the crowd probably just did so through overexcitement or nervous strain. The other strange thing was that people being presented to the royal couple had such little expectation of being spoken to that they either rushed away before the queen or Prince Philip got a chance to stop them or else they made little sense. Eventually, the laughter so embarrassed Prince Philip, or the person he was trying to talk to, that he felt he had to give up the practice.

This leg of the tour was busy, the New Zealanders welcoming wherever we went. On our way out to Hamilton I spotted three painted sheep in a field: one red, one white, and one blue, and later one painted red, white, and blue. There were signs that made us laugh—"God Bless the Queen and Keep an Eye on the Duke" was my favorite. Driving around, we heard "Isn't she *lovely*?" or "Isn't *he* gorgeous?" or with a screech of delight "She waved at *me*!" but what made us smile was the day that the prime minister, Sidney Holland, added his car to the long procession and as we crawled through a small town, a man popped his head into his car and exclaimed, "*Cor!* Bloody old Sid!" We visited the chief of the Waikato tribe, enjoyed flowery and poetic Maori welcomes (though sadly we had to leave just as the *haka* were starting), and watched in amazement as two great war canoes, each over a hundred feet long, carrying one hundred chanting warriors, paddled down the river.

We were now a month and a half into the tour and all of the staff were getting tired and crotchety. I don't know how Prince Philip and the queen survived, continuing to wave as happily as they had done since our arrival—indeed, the queen had developed tremendous muscles in her arm as a result—but they could never relax. On several occasions, when the queen said to her husband, "Look to your right," wanting to point something out to him, he automatically started waving, even if it was to a rather surprised animal minding its own business in a field.

At last, in the New Year, we got two very welcome days off at Moose Lodge near Rotorua—happily far enough away from the horrid sulfurous smell left by the eruption of Mount

Tarawera many years before. I spent them catching up with letters both official and personal, waterskiing with Prince Philip, and rowing around on the lake. From there, we drove 160 miles to Napier, nearly half that distance on dirt roads, the dust conjuring memories of the unsurfaced road trip in Kenya. As the queen and Prince Philip and some of the staff continued onwards by train, Miss Bramford and I traveled by car to Wellington along beautiful avenues of poplars and weeping willows, and the road seemed so inviting that I asked whether I could take over the wheel. There was so little traffic and the roads were so wide and open that I made it in record time, keeping to 80 mph all the way. Pleased with my driving prowess, I was somewhat taken aback when the officials at Government House told me there was a strict 50 mph speed limit throughout New Zealand.

We got through the state opening of Parliament—I felt ludicrous climbing into a long dress and tiara in broad daylight and suffered a fit of nerves at the formality of the event—and then left the dairy farms, weird land formations, and capital city of North Island for the natural grandeur of the mountains, lakes, glaciers, fjords, and sheep farms of South Island. Here the civic reception was lightened by a little dog that ran out of the crowd, leapt up the steps, and when Prince Philip and the queen stood during the presentations, jumped up onto one of the vacant chairs and raised its paw to the crowd as though acknowledging their cheers.

Thankfully, as South Island had many country towns and districts that were inaccessible to our large party, the succession of public welcomes lasted only two days. Most of our remaining time was spent in Christchurch, English in nature, and Dunedin, Scottish, where we were greeted by pipe bands in full Highland dress.

The New Zealand tour was a great success, excellently planned and efficiently executed. It was nothing short of a miracle that, thanks to Sergeant Footman Oulton, not a single piece of luggage had been lost from the stacks that we carried around with us. I had kept up pretty well myself, receiving compliments, via Alice, from the queen, although I had been told off after a very formal dinner party on *Gothic*. The guests had left the large drawing room but the door was not quite closed. I flopped down on a sofa and exclaimed, "What a relief they've all gone!" The queen was very stern. "Pammy, that may be so. But *not* while they might hear." The queen was always impeccable in her behavior and demeanor, performing her duties so perfectly and conscientiously that she always put the rest of us to shame. It was also clear to everyone by now that Prince Philip played an enormous part in the tour's success. I loved his mix of teasing and humor with unexpected kindness and thoughtfulness. It was easy to see why he was so tremendously popular wherever we went. At our farewell party in Invercargill, one of the New Zealand typists said to Alice, "The best investment that the royal family has ever made in all its history is the Duke of Edinburgh."

## ❧ 17 ❧

We spent four days at sea sailing to Sydney. I needed the time to recharge my batteries, for there were going to be as many people in Sydney as there had been in total during the whole month in New Zealand. Our entry into Sydney harbor was unforgettable. It was a glorious day, and the sight of this fantastic harbor with its 150 miles of shoreline was breathtaking. The whole place was alive with small boats, motorboats, speedboats, sailing boats, and ferries festooned with people, and so top-heavy on the side nearest *Gothic* that it seemed preposterous they did not sink. In addition, careering through the tangle, speedboats towed waterskiers in open defiance of the sharks and the more imminent danger of being mown down by other boats, as were the canoeists who had ventured out. In addition to the inevitable church bells and cheering, the sound of the ships' hooters and sirens was deafening. Indeed, sirens hooting in warning were indistinguishable from the hoots of jubilation, and we watched a number of collisions occur.

Eventually, we piled into the procession of cars for the royal progress through the city. In each state visit in Australia we were to have 96 cars with 114 army drivers. After New Zealand it seemed strange to be in an enormous cosmopolitan city with tall buildings and wide streets. There was a tumultuous welcome from the crowds as a shower of streamers, rose petals, and confetti was thrown down from the roofs and windows or straight into the cars by those in the crowd who were near enough. The city was wonderfully decorated, with endless varieties of triumphal arches, including arches made to look like giant crossed boomerangs and even one immense, slowly rotating sham tree trunk.

We plunged headlong into the usual schedule of receptions, inspections, dinners, and drive-throughs. We had all become used to people throwing bunches of flowers into the queen's open car, but in Sydney a new danger presented itself when the overexcited crowd started to throw small flags. The sticks came hurtling in at such speed that they hurt the queen and we were convinced she was going to be blinded. Sydney was abuzz with our visit and we were amused to see women run out of hairdressers' with their hair in pins and nets, the cotton wool that had been protecting their ears from the dryers still in place. We saw men come tumbling out of pubs five minutes before closing time as we drove by, and we were told that this was considered by the authorities to be the greatest triumph of the royal tour. One night we passed a drunk clinging to a lamppost. Prince Philip waved to him and nearly died laughing at the man's agonized expression as he tried to make up his mind whether to wave back or keep his hands safely in place.

As my job demanded, I was very much in the background. In fact so much so that at the Lord Mayor's Ball I was asked to dance, and when I returned to the dais, instead of pushing and shoving my way back, I asked a dignified-looking gentleman if he minded if I passed in front of him. Glaring at me in fury he said, "I most certainly would, young lady. You haven't a hope in hell of queue barging here." I did attract some attention along the way, however. In New Zealand a man had appeared running next to the car shouting for me, as I sat beside the queen driving to a women's lunch, and she asked me who my friend was. Then Johnny returned one evening to report the sighting of a man sitting forlornly on the dais where the civic welcome had taken place earlier. He was muttering disconsolately to himself, and when Johnny drew near he could hear what the man was saying. "Where's Pamela? Why didn't she come? Oh, Pamela, I love you so much. *Why* didn't you come?"

I had been invited by the Osborne family—I had met two of the sons earlier in the tour—to visit their old homestead in Currandooley outside Canberra and rather hoped to take up the offer. As it was Alice's turn for duty that Sunday I didn't think it would matter if I missed church and set off for the sheep station. I had invited Johnny to come with me and we were just getting into the car when Michael sent for him. He came back gloomy, reporting that Michael and Martin insisted we go to church. As the sheep station was thirty miles away, the prospect of this delay completely wrecked our plans for the day. Feeling exactly as though I were back at school, I dashed upstairs and found Michael and Martin sitting at their desks in their morning coats and top hats, their faces like thunder. I received a tremendous lecture about setting the public a good example when one is in the royal entourage and a stern reminder that everyone at Sandringham and Balmoral always went to church. I protested, arguing that if all ten of us turned up in Canberra's tiny church we would displace the locals, who longed for the opportunity to worship with the queen. The secretaries were apoplectic: "Well, then you had better go and tell the archdeacon that you are dead." I protested that the whole point was that I was not dead, intending to be seen very much alive at Currandooley. They told me to "fix it with the archdeacon, then," which of course was their mistake, as I rushed off and spoke to a delighted archdeacon—my space for one of his favorite parishioners—who then thanked me profusely. And so I went off to Currandooley feeling smug and guilty by turns, leaving the others fuming and Johnny being meekly led off to church. Alice couldn't resist telling the queen immediately after the service that I had "got the better of the private secretaries." So strong was the school atmosphere that my small victory was considered a major triumph. Thankfully the sheep station was worth it: stunning countryside, overlooking a lake, and as we rode, white cockatoos flew out of the trees with angry squawks, which reminded me of Michael and Martin.

In Sydney we attended a garden party for eight thousand people at Government House. As usual, several minutes before the queen and Prince Philip were scheduled to emerge to greet the guests, the equerry and I went to stand outside the bedrooms so that the second they emerged we would form a little procession. The queen was always punctual, but this time we waited and waited. No one came to tell us why there was a delay and no one had the faintest idea as to what was causing it. But as soon as the queen came out of her bedroom, I could see why. She looked fantastic, and very different from usual. Instead of the customary Norman Hartnell tight waist and full skirt, she was wearing a sophisticated, pencil-slim white lace dress designed by Hardy Amies. The new look was completed by a black cartwheel picture hat with a transparent brim around which lay four brightly colored feathers. Apparently the delay was caused by the milliner, Aage Thaarup's, large label, which had been clearly visible and was tricky for Bobo to remove. When the queen appeared on the terrace there was an audible gasp from the assembled guests. The Australian fashion correspondents were completely beside themselves and went into a frenzy.

Unusually, I was looking forward to this garden party because my father had written to inform me that Grandpapa's former orderly on board *The Implacable*, back in the early 1900s, was now living in Sydney and had been invited to the garden party. I had made valiant attempts to arrange for him to be presented to Prince Philip, Grandpapa's other grandchild, but been warned by the private secretaries—too professional to bear me any sheep-station grudge—that the list of essential people was already far too long, but they would do their best. When I found out afterwards that Mr. Wallace Bevan had not been presented, I wrote to him saying how sorry I was and that I regretted very much not having had a chance to meet him myself. A few days later I received an enchanting reply in which he explained that he and his wife had been introduced to the queen and in shaking hands had seen me standing just behind her—"in fact we could have touched you when you passed along," he wrote. "I just did not like to worry the officials who were conducting her Majesty." He then described my grandfather as "the most loveable man I have ever met and so understanding. Everyone in *The Implacable* was very fond of him. Of course I had more to do with him than any of the other crew as I was his special Staff Orderly. I was also very much attached to the whole family and I used to escort the family when they went ashore. I had a very special pleasing duty in caring for your father. When he went ashore I carried him most of the time. I also used to carry him up and down the gangway and often took the liberty of taking him forward so the lads could have a look at him. I think he used to enjoy it as young as he was he generally had a very nice broad grin if the boys spoke to him. Oh well, I suppose it would be a bit of a struggle for me now if I had to carry him around. I think he is even taller than his father was and must be fairly heavy." His sentiments were very touching, and I could tell that the glamour of meeting the queen was nothing compared to meeting the grandchildren of his beloved captain.

From Sydney we traveled to Tasmania, and from there set sail for Melbourne. We had been told that this city was contemptuous of Sydney's "Americanism" and that we would find the crowds more restrained and courteous, quite unlike the "dreadful rowdy Sydney crowds." We watched with interest as they tried hard to be reserved but their initial limp waving and embarrassed silence soon gave way to excited cheering that was equal to that in Sydney. We were grateful, however, that they clutched their flags more tightly and didn't try to wriggle under barriers. There was also the occasional very Australian cry of "Good on you, Liz!" and any number of uninhibited "Good on you, Phils." Sometimes there was even a "Good on you, Pam!" and that made me feel pretty special.

At the beginning of March we took the royal train through Victoria, where some of the towns were in the grip of an outbreak of polio. The queen and Prince Philip weren't able to leave the train, instead standing on the observation deck while the speeches were made. On the way back to Melbourne, we all realized how exhausted we were. As the royal couple sat on the observation deck, waiting for the crowds to disperse, I went to see whether they wanted a drink. I found them sitting forlornly on two golden thrones, a brilliant light shining on them in stark contrast to the pitch darkness all around.

They were depressing each other by saying how ghastly the program in Ceylon was going to be and they refused to be cheered up. But I reflected that it was a good sign they could at least see themselves surviving Australia. The strain of the tour was showing—Philip had recently told me that several times in the night he had woken up to find himself very cold, with his right arm outside the bedclothes, and realized that he had been waving to the crowds in his sleep.

In Brisbane, in the strange heat of the tropics, attending the state reception at Parliament House, we found ourselves in a curious maneuver known as "perambulations." Our party formed itself into a long crocodile and we proceeded to wend our way through all the corridors and rooms and along the balconies running round the outside of the building. After completing the somewhat lengthy tour, we found ourselves once more in the chamber, which was still packed with people. Bewilderingly, we then set out again on a second expedition round the buildings, and by the time we had passed through the chamber yet again and were on our third tour I developed the most appalling giggles. Our program had told us, "Perambulations will terminate in the Parliamentary Billiard Room where certain distinguished personages will have assembled for supper." By the time we eventually turned up in the Billiard Room, however, the distinguished personages had obviously abandoned all hope of our ever arriving. The room was thronged with tailcoats, local uniforms, and church dignitaries who were all guzzling ice creams, and our entry passed completely unnoticed. It felt as though we had been doing a sort of stately conga and had come into a room in which the last of the musical chairs had been bagged.

The queen had decided at the beginning of the tour that, even though she loved a good whirl, dancing would be out of the question. She reasoned that if she did dance she would be devoting a considerable amount of time to one man, whereas if she stuck to talking, she would be able to have a few words with a large number. The good people of Brisbane were distraught, however, heartbroken that she had made this decision, and wherever we went we were surrounded by people asking why the queen wouldn't dance. "We don't expect her to dance with us," they said, "but why doesn't she dance with the Duke of Edinburgh? It would be so wonderful to see them dance together." It was funny what people wanted and how they perceived the queen. In Sydney someone had said to me, "I've seen her several times but always sitting in a car. She looked wonderful but it doesn't really count, does it? I mean, it's just like seeing her in a picture. I've simply got to see her *walking*." When I repeated this to Prince Philip he had told me that as a young cadet at Dartmouth he saw King George V drive by and had been surprised that the king's face was not flat, like the postage stamps.

I achieved some notoriety of my own while we were in Brisbane. Having been told about the St. Lucia Water-Ski Club on the river at Brisbane—one of the few shark-free spots, I was informed—I went along at the first opportunity. It was wonderful to be back on the water, alive to the physical exertions of the sport, but being out of practice I suffered some spectacular crashes, and by lunchtime I did not have the strength to climb out of the water onto the low diving board we were using as a pier. As if these humiliations weren't enough, the next edition of the *Brisbane Telegraph* carried a full front-page picture of the tip of my ski and a length of my outstretched arm appearing just above the water. It seemed a rather ignominious way to hit the front pages for the first time, and to make matters worse, I got into terrible trouble with my superiors as it was—apparently—well known that the Brisbane river was a breeding ground for sharks at that time of year.

At last the queen and Prince Philip were allowed to take a break, to go and see the Great Barrier Reef away from the public gaze. Unfortunately, it appeared that the truly amazing sights were to be seen on the outer reefs, but landing on these was considered too dangerous for the queen. We were taken off to tiny Sea Forth Island, where Prince Philip swam around with the men in mask and flippers, but the queen seemed very low. She rarely showed her innermost emotions and was usually so calm and contained. I was worried when I could not even persuade her to explore the island. She cheered up considerably, however, when a boatload of trippers appeared, gesticulating wildly and shouting "Have you seen the queen?!" Suddenly, the queen, in slacks, tore down to the beach, pointed to the other side of the island, and yelled, "She went that way!" As the boat disappeared round the corner, she jumped up and down on the beach with joy.

It was of course vital that the queen and Prince Philip stayed well and healthy. By the time we got to Perth at the end of March, the outbreak of polio had become a major headache for the tour organizers. For a while it was even thought that our visit to Western Australia would have to be canceled because the premier, Mr. Hawke, did not want the responsibility of the queen contracting polio in his state, quite apart from the very real danger of it spreading through large crowds of people and gatherings of children. It was also obvious, however, that if at all possible, the tour must take place. It was decided that we would sleep on board *Gothic* and food from the ship should be sent up to Government House, where we would eat in a separate party. All functions were to be held out of doors, the children's rally canceled, and there was to be no handshaking at any time. The latter proviso was very difficult to adhere to, and the queen soon found herself warmly shaking hands with the Roman Catholic bishop. People had to bob up and down in front of us and I realized just how much the personal contact, that human touch in a handshake, was at the heart of this royal tour and how much it meant to people to be able to say afterwards that they had "touched the queen's dress" or "the queen shook my hand." I was surprised how removed we all felt, and we tried to make up for it by talking that much longer, engaging people in the best way we could.

We left Australia from Fremantle on 1 April 1953. Despite the difficulties of the last part of the tour, this had been a great experience and we had met many interesting people and seen some incredible places. But it was definitely the right time to leave—we were all exhausted after so long, and the press were beginning to have to find new things to say, sniping at us, the original ecstasies overtaken by criticisms. It was a relief to climb back on board *Gothic*, bound for Ceylon.

One of the marvelous aspects of the tour was experiencing the natural beauty of new surroundings. We crossed turquoise waters via the Cocos Islands, palm-treed and set among the coral reefs. The day after leaving we got into the doldrums—not a breath of wind for hours on end—where the sea became completely smooth. Up on deck one evening, as the sun disappeared below the horizon, an emerald-green light spread between the red of the sky and the silver of the sea, and as this light remained for some time after the sun went down, I stood and watched and reflected on how privileged I was to be in this position. The day before we arrived in Ceylon, the ships stopped engines and I went in the barge with the queen and Prince Philip to visit HMS *Ceylon*, which was escorting us on this part of the tour. It was unbearably hot and the queen was nearly boiled alive, so in spite of her protests I held her parasol over her. "I feel like an African queen," she said. "You are an African queen," replied Prince Philip.

As I was about to step into the barge, we spotted a shark cruising around, so I asked the sailor at the bottom of the ladder to hold the parasol while I got in. Conolly came bumbling down the ladder after me and in his anxiety to steady the admiral the sailor dropped the parasol into the sea right on top of the shark. As I knew it would be more than my life was worth to lose it, I was determined to retrieve it, so I waited until the shark had disappeared round the other side of the barge and with the aid of a boat hook and a great deal of patience and dexterity, we managed to succeed in getting it back. Of course, I was teased mercilessly, the story of how I fed the queen's best parasol to a shark in the Indian Ocean everyone's favorite subject for some time.

Arriving in Colombo made me instantly homesick for India. The sights, the sounds, the smells seemed so familiar. I had left Delhi five years earlier, but my time there was still very much a part of me. After disembarking to the traditional mournful greeting played on the drums and conch shells, we made our way to the ceremony of welcome passing a large stand reserved for prep-school boys that was packed with elderly ladies and gentlemen. Later, when we asked why there were so few boys in their stand, we were told that all the other, more enterprising pupils had sold their places for exorbitant sums of money. The opening of Parliament in an open-sided memorial hall was torture for the queen. The coronation dress was very heavy, and when the sun caught all the diamante and metalwork embroidery it became so hot that she was burnt, even through all her stiff petticoats.

I was mesmerized by Ceylon—from the quiet kindness of the people, to the rice fields, the coconut plantations, the large wild mongooses and monkeys, and the staggering "Fortress in the Sky," a gigantic flat-topped rock rising over four hundred feet above the surrounding countryside, upon which King Kashyapa in the fifth century had built a fabulous impregnable fortress city covering three acres, complete with gardens and exquisite buildings. Even the disastrously rainy parties, during which guests had to scamper for shelter every time torrential showers threatened to ruin their finery, were manageable. At dusk one evening, as we watched the flying foxes and deep, dark-black clouds gather over the Governor's House, we were diverted by a noise of jingling bells as a beaming Prince Philip arrived with nine elephants he had managed to waylay for the queen to see.

In Kandy we stayed in the King's Pavilion, where my father had lived when his HQ was in Ceylon. I remembered all the stories he had told me, and it was such fun to see where it had all happened. As we waved good-bye to our hosts, it was very clear from the hospitality and warmth we had been shown that "the Queen of Sri Lanka" took pride of place in the country and was a valued successor to a monarchy that had existed since 543 BC.

We headed back to England via Aden, Uganda, Malta, and Gibraltar. Aden was weirdly beautiful—towering dark-gray volcanic rocks splitting the horizon with their peaks as we came into the harbor early one morning. This was the first place in which the queen had been greeted by groups of black-robed women emitting their shrill, trilling cry of welcome. On the last night aboard *Gothic* we dined quietly by ourselves and after supper the queen knighted the captain. Michael had taken him aside and warned him that after she had tapped him on one shoulder he must on no account get up but remain kneeling while she tapped him on the other. He must have thought that this warning was to save him from mortal wounding and that he was going to be struck with the sharp edge of the sword, because the queen said later that she almost had to chase him round the cabin to get him to kneel and that when she raised the sword he flinched and looked at her in considerable alarm.

We left *Gothic* at 4 a.m. on 28 April, all of us extremely sad. We had been such a united party for the past five months and it seemed wrong to be breaking up so near the end of the tour and having *Gothic* denied the triumphant return home. The newly commissioned royal yacht *Britannia* had now been completed, and having taken Prince Charles and Princess Anne out to Malta, was coming to Tobruk so that the queen and Prince Philip could set sail in her.

Having stopped over in Entebbe we flew to El Adem and then drove to Tobruk, where we went straight on board *Britannia*. Our regrets at leaving *Gothic* were soon forgotten in the extreme comfort in which we now found ourselves. Several senior members of the household at Buckingham Palace had come out in her and a new equerry replaced Johnny, who had flown home to organize his wedding to Frances Roche (they were to become the parents of Princess Diana). They were good company but inevitably they brought the rather stiff formality of Buckingham Palace with them and the spirit of the family party that had toured the world together was broken. It was a joy for the queen and Prince Philip to be reunited with their children. At our Sunday church service, Conolly read the prayer for the royal family, "We humbly beseech Thee to bless our gracious Queen, Elizabeth the Queen Mother, Philip Duke of Edinburgh, Charles Duke of Cornwall and all the Royal Family." When he came to the end Princess Anne's furious small voice was heard, "He hasn't prayed for me, Mummy," thereby nearly bringing the service to an end as we all laughed so much.

It was lovely for me to hear of all the children's adventures staying with "Uncle Dickie and Aunt Edwina" in Malta. They brought me a letter from my mother telling me that poor little Neola had died from kidney failure. I was very sad because I had expected to be back with him in Malta in a couple of weeks' time. They wanted to hear about the mischief he had caused, so I told them the story of the time their mother had been staying with us at Broadlands. "Pammy," she said, "I am quite fond of Neola and I don't mind him coming into my bedroom. I don't even mind him opening my box of chocolates. But must he take a bite out of every single one of them?"

We were joined at sea by the Mediterranean Fleet, two hundred miles from Malta. Fifteen ships now joined the four frigates already escorting us, including my father on board his flagship, the cruiser *Glasgow*. With perfect timing, all the ships fired a royal salute, wheeling inwards and steaming past *Britannia*, the ships' companies lining the decks and giving three cheers and the big ships parading guards and bands. They passed by us at no more than half a cable's distance, throwing *Britannia* about with their swell and giving Conolly apoplexy. As the ships followed within one and a half cables—less than three hundred meters—of each other, their bows tore through the white foam of the wake of the ship ahead. It was magnificent and thrilling to watch, and from then on, whenever anything spectacular was done, it was known as "doing a Dickie."

The "great man" himself transferred to *Britannia* by jack-stay to report the fleet to the sovereign, and following the queen's invitation my father remained on board. Of course he took charge of everything, and within the space of a few minutes he had assumed the roles of private secretary, press secretary, equerry, lady-in-waiting, master of the household, and nurse. After lunch he had us hopping about watching three of the Mediterranean Fleet submarines diving; jet aircraft flying off HMS *Eagle*; a flypast of Avengers and Skyraiders, as well as Shackletons from RAF Luqa. My father stayed in the guest cabin opposite mine, which had an adjoining sitting room in which Charles had been doing his lessons. He had to move his books and remarked to me very solemnly, "Uncle Dickie is a nuisance."

When we reached Malta, *Britannia* steamed up between the lines of her escorting ships, accompanied above by noisy helicopters. We reduced speed and just outside the Grand Harbour breakwater we were met by my father's big barge. As it heaved up and down in rough water, my mother leapt on board in her usual nimble style. Talking had to wait as we were instantly caught up in the whirl of a flypast of jets. Then all the ships in harbor, the naval shore establishments, and the saluting batteries fired a royal salute and, passing the breakwater, *Britannia* was escorted to her berth by landing craft. The noise was deafening—cheering from the packed crowds, the ringing of church bells, the klaxon of ships' sirens, all drowned out by the noise of firecrackers, which even by Maltese standards were phenomenal and fearsome.

It felt so good to be back in Malta, to see my parents and be surrounded by familiar things at Admiralty House. The queen, Prince Philip, and Alice dined that night with us before going on to a ball at the Phoenicia. At last the queen was able to dance. I felt even happier for her the next day as she and Prince Philip were able to snatch a small opportunity to act as normal parents and take the children for a drive around the island in their small car.

There were still official engagements to attend in Malta, so I remained on board *Britannia*. The Maltese nobility were in their element at the state ball, where they danced their famous *maltija* in powdered wigs and eighteenth-century costumes. It was so windy that the queen and I were nearly blown off the flight deck of the aircraft carrier *Eagle*, and the archbishop got so cold during the final brilliant firework display that my mother had to wrap her striped silk stole around him. We sailed out of Malta to a terrific send-off from the crowd, people cheering and waving from every possible vantage point. I went up on deck to watch us come into Gibraltar harbor, to gaze at the massive outline of the Rock and to remind myself that this was another part of the tour. Being back in Malta with my parents had given me a false feeling that the tour was over. My spirits were lifted when we went to see the apes—fifty of them guarded by the army, no doubt because of the saying that when the apes leave the Rock the British will leave too. We fed them peanuts as the press photographers pressed themselves against the apes' sleeping cages with their cameras poking through the bars. No one made any jokes.

As we entered the English Channel, the Mediterranean Fleet parted company, steaming past at twenty-five knots with their customary flourish and precision. Off Yarmouth in the Isle of Wight, the prime minister, Winston Churchill, came on board and, rather alarmingly, the queen put me on the other side of him during dinner. He put me at my ease, however, by showing me the fob watch that my great-grandfather, Ernest

Cassell, had given him. He brought us up to date on the no-
torious case in which a Russian spy, Vladimir Petrov, and his
wife, from the Soviet embassy in Canberra, had defected and
secured political asylum in Australia a couple of weeks after
we had left. As he said good night to the queen, she said, "I
hope you sleep well." He looked at her and replied, "Now we
have got you home, ma'am, I shall sleep very well."

Coming up to Tower Bridge, festooned with a "Welcome
Home" sign, we held our breath as we passed underneath,
for it seemed *impossible* that there would be room for
*Britannia*'s masts. At lunch, with a twinkle in her eye, the
queen resolutely remained in her slacks while she entertained
the Queen Mother and Princess Margaret, who were rather
splendidly arrayed in silks and diamonds. After lunch the
queen went below to her cabin to change. When she came
back up on deck she was extra specially smart and appeared
rather pleased with herself. She saw me looking and said quietly, "I kept these things aside so that I would have something
new to wear for our arrival in London." At Westminster Pier,
we disembarked to a host of dignitaries, but there was no
one more important to me in that crowd than my sister, who,
touchingly, was there to welcome me home. Rather thrillingly, Alice, Michael, Martin, and I had to travel through
the cheering crowds to the palace behind the state landau,
in a carriage drawn by four bay horses. I was bursting with
pleasure and excitement—for me that carriage drive made
the relentless pace of the past six months worthwhile. We
started out in solemn silence but were soon reduced to fits
of giggles—as the men were sitting with their backs to the
horses they had to rely on Alice and me to warn them whenever we were approaching colors so that they could swiftly
doff their hats the moment we alerted them.

The Grand Hall of the palace was lined with gentlemen-at-arms and yeomen of the guard and more courtiers than I should have thought existed, and seeing tea laid out and watching everyone move about in that stiff Buckingham Palace sort of way, it was difficult to believe I had actually just traveled around the world. I took one look at the room buzzing around me and realized that with immediate effect I could lead a normal life again without having to attend an opening of Parliament every few days, or having to climb into a long evening dress, tiara, and gloves nearly every night. I felt an overwhelming urge to escape, so I located my luggage and fled.

# ～ *Epilogue* ～

After our return to England, the next five years of my life were largely uneventful, with none of the spectacular events that I had been swept up in before.

Of course, like any young girl of my age, I fell in and out of love—romances that were serious at the time, some even lasting a couple of years—and I received ten proposals of marriage. However, I never felt deeply enough in love to accept any of them.

At the age of twenty-eight, I experienced a period of introspection and quiet despair, which was not helped by a nasty bout of Asian flu. I thought myself to be a "nothing." I wanted to be a writer and yet I wasn't writing anything worth reading. I even stopped writing my diary—something that I had kept up pretty much since the age of seven.

Instead I spent a considerable amount of time carrying out official engagements. I was invited to serve as patron or president of a number of local, county, or national organizations including the Royal London Society for the Blind; the Embroiderers' Guild (inappropriate as I didn't embroider but it proved impossible to refuse such determined ladies); the Music Circle of the Royal Overseas League (even more inappropriate but they had a chairman who point-blank refused to take no for an answer); member of the International Council of the United World Colleges (no chance of saying no to the president, my father); and—again, coerced by my father— I became the commandant of the Girls' Nautical Training Corps (I felt ridiculous walking across station concourses on my way to their events, dressed in mock admiral's regalia). I particularly enjoyed being president of the Southampton International Youth Rally and launching HMS *Bossington*. Otherwise it was mostly single engagements such as opening the first comprehensive school in Southampton, lecturing at Women's Institutes on subjects such as Tonga, and the usual church fêtes. I divided my time between Broadlands and a small converted garage flat in the mews off Wilton Crescent, taking in plays, films, and exhibitions when in London.

Despite all these duties, I could tell that my parents were slightly unsettled by my inability to wholeheartedly embrace public and social life and find my niche. Then, one evening, in 1959, I went to a cocktail party in Chelsea. A man—who, as a friend later said, resembled a Greek god—came over to talk to me, monopolizing me for the entire evening. I was completely bowled over. This man was the designer David Hicks. It was an unorthodox match but one that would change my life completely. After twenty-nine years as the dutiful daughter of a family at the heart of British society, with all its traditions and ceremonies, I was about to enter a completely new world—of fashion, design, and the whirlwind of the 1960s. And unorthodox though the match may have been, our marriage was to last thirty-eight years.

As we flew back from our honeymoon, a steward came over to David and whispered that we would be disembarking from the airplane first. Mystified, we could only assume we would need guiding through the frenzy of waiting press—there had been an astonishing amount of interest in our engagement and wedding—though I thought it pretty extraordinary that six weeks later there should still be even an *iota* of interest in us.

As we landed, however, and saw a crowd of newspaper reporters and photographers on the tarmac, we were sure our assumption had been correct. John was waiting for us at the bottom of the steps and I felt grateful to my brother-in-law for coming to help navigate our way through the press. But as we left the airplane I could see that there was something in his demeanor that didn't quite match the lightheartedness of the occasion—after all we were only coming back from our honeymoon—and we were pushed rather unceremoniously by a steward into a car and driven to a nearby VIP room.

My mother had died. On a tour of the Far East to inspect branches of St. John's Ambulance and Save the Children, after a hard day forcing herself to undertake inspections and attend a reception while feeling dreadfully unwell, she went to bed on the point of collapse. She died in the night from a stroke. She was fifty-eight years old.

When I heard the words that John was saying, they made no sense to me at all and he had to repeat them several times before I could take them in and understand their terrible meaning.

My mother had left instructions that on her death she should like to be buried at sea. Three days later, her body returned home and was sent to rest in Romsey Abbey. On Thursday, 25 February, a gray and blustery day, my father, Patricia, John, David, and I drove to Portsmouth and alongside Prince Philip and his mother we boarded the frigate HMS *Wakeful*. My sister and I were numb but Aunt Alice, as ever, was intensely emotional. About twelve miles out to sea, the Archbishop of Canterbury, Geoffrey Fisher, led prayers as my mother's coffin, draped with a Union Jack, slipped into the sea to the sound of twelve bosun pipes, and finally the last post and reveille. My father, wearing his uniform of an admiral of the fleet, stood with tears streaming down his face, staring at the spot where the coffin had disappeared. It was the only time I had ever seen him weep. He then kissed his wreath before throwing it out to sea. Prince Philip, Patricia, and I cast ours into the water and I clung to David for the comfort I now needed so badly.

Waiting a respectful distance away was the Indian frigate INS *Trishal*, and as we steamed away she took our place and, on Panditji's instructions, marigolds were scattered upon the waves.

# *Acknowledgments*

My loving thanks to my daughter, India, for her constant encouragement and criticism, and to my son, Ashley, who gave me the title, although I suspect he meant it as a joke.

I am grateful to my sister, Patricia Mountbatten, for helping me with memories of our childhood. And to Anne Bradstock for memories of our school days, and to Jaya Thadani for memories of India.

A sincere thank-you to Gillian Stern for her work in bringing the book into shape and making it readable. And to Kate Oldfield and Eugenie Furniss and my editor, Kirsty Dunseath, for her patience.

# Acknowledgments

# About the Author

The daughter of Lord Louis and Edwina Mountbatten, LADY PAMELA HICKS was lady-in-waiting to Queen Elizabeth II both when she was a princess and following her coronation. In the 1960s she married the designer David Hicks, who became internationally celebrated. This is Pamela Hicks's second book; her first, *India Remembered*, was published in 2007.